To Jack:

Joyous Christmas!

I praise our Lord

for you and all

you have done

to help share

His love...

Joel

THE HEART OF GOD

The Heart of God

By

Lloyd John Ogilvie

Published by Regal Books
A Division of Gospel Light
Ventura, California, U.S.A.
Printed in U.S.A.

Regal Books is a ministry of Gospel Light, an evangelical Christian publisher dedicated to serving the local church. We believe God's vision for Gospel Light is to provide church leaders with biblical, user-friendly materials that will help them evangelize, disciple and minister to children, youth and families.

It is our prayer that this Regal Book will help you discover biblical truth for your own life and help you meet the needs of others. May God richly bless you.

For a free catalog of resources from Regal Books/Gospel Light please contact your Christian supplier or call 1-800-4-GOSPEL.

The devotional readings in this book are based on *The Autobiography of God* by Lloyd John Ogilvie, Regal Books, © 1979.

Library of Congress Cataloging-in-Publication Data
Ogilvie, Lloyd John.
The heart of God / Lloyd John Ogilvie.
p. cm.
ISBN 0-8307-1656-4
1. God—Knowableness—Prayer-books and devotions—English.
2. Christian life. I. Title.
BT 102.0354 1994 94-27433
231.7—dc20 CIP

1 2 3 4 5 6 7 8 9 10 11 12 13 14 15 / 00 99 98 97 96 95 94

Contents

Part II
Living in Light of the Kingdom

Part III
Riches in the Lord's Treasury

Part IV
Growing in the Lord's Vineyard

Introduction

We all long for the power to live life to the fullest. We need power to love, forgive and serve. Often we feel a lack of power to live what we believe and to be faithful, bold disciples.

A deeper issue is involved, however; it is the issue of authority. God entrusts His power to those who have accepted His absolute authority over their lives.

Jesus' central teaching in His parables is about how to live our lives in the kingdom of God under the authority of God as King. The Master's most gripping teaching is often prefaced by statements such as, "The kingdom of God is like...." Then, in the most impelling ways, Jesus reveals aspects of the nature of God our King and of the kingdom of God as the reign and rule of God in our minds and hearts, our relationships and responsibilities, and in the issues of righteousness and justice in society. We discover the kingdom of God is within us, between us and in every realm of life.

The power of God—the King of the universe, our world and our lives—is given to those who accept Christ as Lord and the Holy Spirit as the source of strength. When we live under the authority of God our

King, we can know this limitless flow of power. The King has a plan and purpose for us. When we seek and do His will as Sovereign of our lives, we are provided supernatural resources.

The kingdom of God is now; it is unfolding in the immediate future, and it will be gloriously revealed in the end of time. Living under the reign of the King in the kingdom of God maximizes the present, gives us clear direction and goals for our tomorrows and provides us with confidence for our ultimate destiny in heaven.

Nothing is more important than knowing the King of the Kingdom personally and intimately. The parables help us to know Him as our Father. *More than an aloof ruler of our lives, Jesus reveals His heart.* Thus, the title of this book, *The Heart of God.*

We discover that the Father's authority is always coupled with His grace; judgment is given with an opportunity for forgiveness. The parables of Jesus about the kingdom of God enable us to pray, "Your kingdom come, Your will be done" with greater appreciation of what we are asking and the nature of the One whose authority we accept.

Daily, hourly, we affirm the only liberating answer to the persistent question, "Who's in charge here?" We accept that God our Father who is King is not only in charge, but also demands our obedience. Control issues are settled and the quest for human power over people and situations is overcome as we receive authentic spiritual power to serve. The nemesis of our nature—to be self-serving—is replaced by a dominant desire to serve the King of our lives and serve others as He guides the way and provides the power.

The devotional readings in this book dwell on this challenging aspect of living—today—in the kingdom of God. Each chapter will give you an aspect of life as it was meant to be lived, daring to claim the glory and the power of the Kingdom and to appropriate them in everyday living.

The parables are so packed with meaning that we will use two, sometimes three, devotional chapters to probe the meaning and the application of each one. Note that the Scripture readings at the beginning of each chapter are excerpts from the parable. You may prefer to refer to the whole parable in the Bible and to read it in its entirety.

As you use this book, whether in your private devotionals or in a group, I invite you to allow yourself to be drawn into the setting of each parable. The questions at the end of each chapter will assist you in thinking through applying to your own life the one central theme of each parable. These questions can also serve as discussion starters for a small group or a class. The Discussion Leader's Guide at the end of the book will also help to guide you in your discussion groups.

Often we use the phrase, "In light of that...." The

goal of this book is to provide both the light of understanding and the illumination of the priorities of authentic power. To live in the light of the Kingdom provides both. The abundant life really begins when we accept the authority, receive the power of the King and live in the kingdom of God. It's a delight to share this adventure with you through this book.

Lloyd Ogilvie

Part I

My Father, the King

1

Escape from Paradise

SCRIPTURE READING:

A certain man had two sons; and the younger of them said to his father, "Father, give me the share of the estate that falls to me." And he divided his wealth between them. And not many days later, the younger son gathered everything together and went on a journey into a distant country, and there he squandered his estate with loose living.

LUKE 15:11-13

We too easily characterize the lost son in the parable of the prodigal son as the offscouring of humanity—drunks, dope addicts, sexual indulgences, criminals. But if we look closely, we may catch sight of ourselves in this longing to leave our true home and to wander away to a far country.

Note that the younger son kept his real agenda hidden when he asked his father for his share of the inheritance. He did not say, "So I can get out of here and run my own life!" Why would the younger son want to leave such a father? The father showed no hint of harshness. No rigid dictator, this father. He longed only for his sons to enjoy the fruit of his labors and careful accumulation dependent on him.

Linger for a moment on the meaning of our inheritance from our heavenly Father: the resources of life; intellect, emotion, will; healthy bodies and a beautiful world filled with the delights of existence. Enjoy! But with one qualification: that we acknowledge they are gifts and that we praise the Giver.

There's the problem. We want to claim them as our own, without Him, and live the lie that what we are and have are the result of our own clever creativity. It is a problem as old as Adam and Eve, this lust to escape from paradise, this stupidity of independence. Many of us are not squanderers with problems but just wanderers from our potential. Like the younger son, we have to prove ourselves to ourselves. We all want to be the one thing we can never be: god over our own lives.

There's a word for that; it has lots of synonyms, but at the root it is "sin." Although the younger son committed sin, there was one taproot sin of willful rebellion: independence. The desire to be great on his own.

The far country is the realm of rebellion. More than geography, it is a condition of the soul. It may be a total rejection of a faith that was once warm and dynamic. Or it may be relationships, priorities or involvements that focus on our self-indulgence or aggrandizement. These are aspects of every one of us who would escape the bosom of the Father and dwell in the land of self-will.

Most of us drift from paradise. Little things at first. Then our plans. Soon our money. Before long, our deepest relationships. Finally, our hearts. We are no longer at home with God. His guidance for life's decisions begins to seem irrelevant. We are intimidated by others who speak of intimacy with God. Too emotional. God is "up there." What is down here becomes our far country.

But in vain we travel afar in search of freedom or anything or anyone to fill our emptiness. We have no nostrums for the incurable homesickness for the Father, but we try to find them. Success, position, recognition, accumulation—like the lost son, we use good things inordinately for the wrong reason. And they are no substitute for what we enjoyed with the Father.

Fortunately, this parable also describes how to return to paradise. We must come to ourselves. This means we must see ourselves as we are, and that isn't always easy. Some of us resist it as long as we can. It may take a tragedy, or the loss of a cherished relationship or the disintegration of our carefully erected defense mechanism to make us realize that we are feeding on husks in the far country.

But the beauty of this parable is that it shows that when we see ourselves for what we are, we can also see what we may yet become. Thomas Wolfe was wrong. We *can* go home again. We *can* return to paradise!

Kingdom Thinking

1. Why is it sometimes hard to confess our dependency on God? Have you found that particular areas of your own life are difficult to turn over to Him?

2. At times, we all drift from a close relationship with God our Father. From your own experience and observation of others, what are the major causes? Describe some of the more "respectable" far countries in which people live away from the Father.

3. What does this parable tell us about the nature of God our Father? What attributes stand out? Which ones mean most to you? Why?

Related Readings

1 Corinthians 6:9-11 2 Corinthians 5:16-21
Galatians 5:1

Prayer to the King

We praise You, King of our lives, for the riches of our inheritance in Your kingdom. We confess our dependence upon You; it is in You that we live and move and have our being. Keep us from lusting for false freedom in far countries. Through Jesus Christ our Lord, Amen.

2

Lavish Love

SCRIPTURE READING:

The father said to his slaves, "Quickly bring out the best robe and put it on him, and put a ring on his hand and sandals on his feet; and bring the fattened calf, kill it, and let us eat and be merry; for this son of mine was dead, and has come to life again; he was lost, and has been found." And they began to be merry.

LUKE 15:22-24

Although this story has become famous as the parable of the prodigal son, the spotlight is really on the father. He is on center stage the moment the curtain goes up, and even when he is offstage he dominates the scene. The two sons are but supporting characters, vivid contrasts to the father. Change the scenery and the father's gracious love still thunders through. He speaks both when delivering his eloquent lines and when he silently waits.

Who is the father? Jesus hoped we would ask. The father is God, and God is the real prodigal. This King is more than a ruler, He is a lover, and to live in His kingdom is to be loved lavishly. This is the parable of the prodigal God!

Shocking? Perhaps. But read Jesus' amazing drama again in Luke 15:11-32. Then check the definition of "prodigal." It means extravagant, lavish, unrestrained, copious. This describes the father more than the sons. Their negative prodigality is set in bold relief to the creative prodigality of the father.

Jesus portrays the father in this way in order to tell us what God is like. The father's lavish love that accepts returning prodigals and pouting sons knows no limits. His forgiveness knows no boundaries, his joy no restraint. We look at the father in the parable and behold what God was doing and would do through Jesus. It would mean Golgotha, but would never end there. Wasteful? Lavish, extravagant, excessive? Yes! Especially when you consider the disastrous defection and the ultraviolence of humankind. Why track him in the corridors of conscience in the far country? Why this in-spite-of love? What did we do to deserve that? Nothing. That's the mystery and wonder of it all. But we need love, forgiveness and reconciliation more than we need breathing, food or sleep. That's what God offers because that's what He is: the prodigal God.

The father in Jesus' parable shows his prodigality in several startling ways. In the first place, the younger son would never have asked for his share of the inheritance if he had been uncertain about the response. In the second place, the father let the son go. He knew that love only possesses what it releases. We feel the wrenching agony of the separation, the good-byes that leave so much unsaid. Many of us have packed up our own share of the inheritance and have left the Father as if we plan never to come back. Do we know that we have broken God's heart?

We recall the depths of the young son's descent into the far country of rebellion. He ended up as a Hebrew feeding swine, which his ancient religion abhorred. He was so hungry he was willing to eat the carob pods the forbidden beasts refused. It was then that he came to himself, seeing himself as he really was. It was then that he was able to return home and to say, "Father, I have sinned against heaven, and in your sight" (Luke 15:18).

The father's lavish love was not misplaced by shielding his son from the hard reality of sin. No dispatched guardians were standing by to soften the blows of coming to himself. Prodigal love again! So often I hear people ask if God sends difficulties. He doesn't have to. Life offers more than enough. We cry out, "What's the meaning of this, God?" He patiently waits until we can humbly ask, "What's the meaning *in* this, God?"

The parable then tells us what kind of prodigal love awaits us each time, every time, we return to the Father. He has been waiting, watching, longing for us. Behold your God! This is our God who sees us returning from a long way off, and runs to meet us. It was considered very undignified for a senior man to run. But look at prodigal love give wings to the father's feet. He can't run fast enough; his legs won't respond quickly enough to express the expectant longing of his heart to welcome his son home.

After the grand celebration, welcoming the young son, the truth about God's lavish love must surely come home to us. Whatever else we believe about God, we can't miss this. *He runs to us.* Our least response unleashes His lavish love. Right now, He is running to meet us and to enfold us in His arms!

Kingdom Thinking

1. Consider the elder brother's reaction in Luke 15:25-30. Was the father's lavish love actually the cause of the elder brother's attitude?

2. Why is jealousy out of place when we see grace lavished upon people who have sinned?

3. Can you cite from experience an example of love that lets go, although it is painful?

Related Readings

Psalm 103:8-14 Matthew 20:1-16 Ephesians 2:1-10

Prayer to the King

Thank You, dear Father, for Your extravagant love! You give seed to the sower and bread to the eater—even when we do not acknowledge Your gifts. While we were yet sinners, You sent Your Son to die for us. And You empower us to love others, in light of Your love. For Your lavish love, we praise You through Christ our Lord, Amen.

3

All We Like Sheep

SCRIPTURE READING:

What man among you, if he has a hundred sheep and has lost one of them, does not leave the ninety-nine in the open pasture, and go after the one which is lost, until he finds it? And when he has found it, he lays it on his shoulders, rejoicing. And when he comes home, he calls together his friends and his neighbors, saying to them "Rejoice with me, for I have found my sheep which was lost!" I tell you that in the same way, there will be more joy in heaven over one sinner who repents, than over ninety-nine righteous persons who need no repentance.

LUKE 15:4-7

From my hotel room overlooking the Atlantic in Ocean City, New Jersey, I could see the endless streams of people walking up and down the busy boardwalk. I was preparing a sermon on the parable of the lost sheep when I heard a disturbing announcement over the loudspeaker near the boardwalk:

"A little girl about five years old, answering to the name of Wendy, has been lost. She is wearing a yellow dress and carrying a teddy bear. She has brown eyes, auburn hair. Anyone knowing the whereabouts of Wendy, please report to the Music Pier. Her parents are waiting for her here."

I tried to return to my reading, but my mind was on Wendy. How did she feel without the clasp of her father's strong hand? I pictured her parents. What must they be feeling?

A question from the Pharisees prompted the parable of the lost sheep. The Pharisees had criticized Jesus for the company He kept. His love and vulnerability had attracted a needy group of friends: abhorred tax collectors, irreligious people, nonpracticing Jewish outcasts, morally suspicious failures. "Why spend your time with them, Jesus?" the Pharisees demanded to know. His answer was not defensive. He told them about God in a way that answers our deepest questions and lances our infected conceptions.

Sheep and shepherds were a part of life in Palestine. A hundred sheep would be a sign of prosperity. But what kind of shepherd would leave ninety-nine of them to search for one gone astray? Would that be good business? Why not cut your losses and get on with caring about the flock? Why is *one sheep* so important?

Israel considered herself the flock of God. Every worshiping Hebrew had said or sung Psalm 100 countless times: "We are His people and the sheep of His pasture" (v. 3). But the concern was whether any of these sneering, scoffing Pharisees ever identified with Isaiah's confession: "All of us like sheep have gone astray, each of us has turned to his own way; but the Lord has caused the iniquity of us all to fall on Him" (Isa. 53:6). And did any of those who considered themselves shepherds over Israel remember Ezekiel 34? "Thus says the Lord God, 'Behold, I am against the shepherds, and I shall demand My sheep from them....Behold, I Myself will search for My sheep and seek them out'" (vv. 10,11).

What a contrast with the saying the Pharisees had among themselves: "There is a joy before God when those who provoke Him perish from the world." Jesus said, "The Son of Man has come to seek and to save that which was lost" (Luke 19:10). In His kingdom, the joy is in the one sheep who returns to the fold, the one sinner who repents. And we can be sure that the searching Shepherd has put it into our hearts to long to return to Him. As Pascal said, "Thou wouldst not be searching for me hadst I not already found thee." This is implied in Francis Thompson's "Hound of Heaven":

I fled Him, down the nights and down the
days;
I fled Him, down the arches of the years;
I fled Him, down the labyrinthine ways
Of my own mind; and in the mist of tears
I hid from Him, and under running laughter
Up vistaed hopes I sped;
And shot, precipitated,
Adown Titanic glooms of chasmed fears.
From those strong feet that followed,
followed after.

That was Francis Thompson's flight and plight. But skip down to the last stanza of his poem and hear the Shepherd say,

Ah, fondest, blindest, weakest
I am He whom thou seekest![1]

It is true. All our longing, restlessness and discontent are because of our search for the One who has found us.

And the Shepherd's staff? It is in the shape of a cross! Seeking the sheep, and finding it, He hoists it upon His shoulders and carries us home. Think of it! God Himself carrying us home. The arms that were stretched out on a cross are yet strong enough to carry us. We have carried the burden of being lost. Now that He has found us, He forever carries us!

Kingdom Thinking

1. As a parent, have you ever experienced the panic of realizing that one of your children is lost? What emotions in such a parent's heart do you think God shares over His lost sheep? If you are not a parent, have you ever felt deeply the pain over someone who is acting as though he or she is lost?

2. In what ways can you identify with the lost sheep?

3. What does it really mean to be lost spiritually? What are some symptoms of being estranged from God?

4. What broken relationships among people may reflect the deeper problem of a broken relationship with God?

Related Readings

Psalm 78:51-55 Luke 19:1-10 2 Corinthians 7:8-16

Prayer to the King

Shepherd of our souls, we are lost without You. Help us to so rejoice in Your presence that we do not think of straying. Thank You for Your seeking love that finds us. Thank You for the arms of Jesus, strong enough to bear our sins, gentle enough to fold us to His breast.
In His name, Amen.

Note

1. Francis Thompson, "The Hound of Heaven."

4

Coin of the Realm

SCRIPTURE READING:

Or what woman, if she has ten silver coins and loses one coin, does not light a lamp and sweep the house and search carefully until she finds it? And when she has found it, she calls together her friends and neighbors, saying "Rejoice with me, for I have found the coin which I had lost!" In the same way, I tell you, there is joy in the presence of the angels of God over one sinner who repents.

LUKE 15:8-10

After the parable of the lost sheep, Jesus moves to a second illustration of the nature of the King over the kingdom of God: the parable of the lost coin.

Why such consternation over one coin worth about twenty cents in our money? Even if it constituted a day's wages at the time of Christ, more is implied here than the monetary value of the coin.

The women of Jesus' time wore a frontlet on their brow called a *semedi*. It was made up of ten coins, signifying a woman's betrothal or marriage relationship. A loss of one coin from the frontlet would be traumatic. More than the symmetry of the frontlet, it was significant of the fellowship the woman had with her beloved. It was not just the loss of the cosmetic beauty, but also the careless loss of the completed symbol of her lover's gift that would alarm the woman. That's why she searched for the coin so feverishly. She had to find it! It meant everything to her.

The search was not easy. The dirt floors of the homes in Palestine were overlaid with straw. Seldom were there windows to illuminate the one-room dwellings. A low door afforded little help. A lamp must be lighted to aid in the long search through the straw and dust.

But the coin must be found! The careful sweeping and sifting expresses the woman's concern. The lost coin is sought with undiminishable persistence. If a woman would do that to restore her frontlet, what will God do to restore us to fellowship? Everything! Nothing is too much, no search too long, no obstruction too great. The point of the parable shows how God loves and searches for you and me much more than He would search for a coin.

Allow the healing balm of that truth to soak into the crevices of your heart. The Lord of the universe, who came as a seeking, suffering Savior, who comes to us in the longing love of the Holy Spirit, will not be put off or dissuaded. We have no "safe" place to hide. He knows who and where we are. He wants to heal that negative self-depreciation that naggingly wonders why He has time or concern for us.

Both the parable of the lost sheep and the parable of the lost coin end on the same triumphant note: Joy. And Jesus wants no misunderstanding: "In the same way, I tell you, there is joy in the presence of the angels of God over one sinner who repents" (Luke 15:10). It is as though He asks, "Do you want joy? There is no other way than to share God's joy over the recovery of the lost."

Recently, a woman said to me, "I've lost the excitement of being a Christian." She confessed that she had known joy while she was astounded by how much God loved her in spite of her failures and selfishness. She also related the delight she used to have in sharing with others what had happened to her so they might know what she had experienced. The more we talked, the more a simple diagnosis became clear: She was no longer amazed, and she was not caring for people.

Joy is the outward expression of the inner experience of grace. This woman's "dis-grace" was her lack of fellowship with the Lord and a refusal to talk about her faith with those who desperately needed to know that the Shepherd had found them. Her joy returned when she once again opened her heart to the startling and ultimately satisfying good news of the Cross and what God had done for her. This renewed her passion for people and their needs.

In the preceding chapter, I related the incident of the little girl who was lost, and then found, along the boardwalk in Ocean City, New Jersey. As I closed the Bible that night, my heart was flooded with almost uncontainable exuberance about my Lord. I knew that the joy I experienced would last only as long as my purpose and passion centered on the lost on the boardwalk, or on the streets of Los Angeles, or in the pews of my church or in the homes of my parish.

The joy of the Lord is ours when we have the same concern for others that the woman in this parable had for the lost coin.

Kingdom Thinking

1. Reflect back on how you felt when you first realized God's love for you personally. How have your feelings about your relationship with Him changed since then? Have the changes been for better or worse?

2. Have you ever been involved in leading anyone to Christ, or talking with him or her about God's love? What feelings about your own relationship with Him did this experience stir?

3. If you haven't had such an experience, can you think of someone who may need the message of the

Kingdom? Project the joy you could experience by sharing your own experience with that person.

Related Readings

Psalm 139:7-12 Jeremiah 29:11-14 Matthew 6:25-33

Prayer to the King

How we cherish the knowledge that You value us,
O Lord! Help us to value ourselves as You do.
Help us to value others enough to know the joy of
sharing with them how much You love them.
Through Jesus Christ our Lord, Amen.

5

The Midnight Visitor

SCRIPTURE READING:

Suppose one of you shall have a friend, and shall go to him at midnight, and say to him, "Friend, lend me three loaves; for a friend of mine has come to me from a journey, and I have nothing to set before him"; and from inside he shall answer and say, "Do not bother me; the door has already been shut and my children and I are in bed; I cannot get up and give you anything." I tell you, even though he will not get up and give him anything because he is his friend, yet because of his persistence he will get up and give him as much as he needs.

LUKE 11:5-8

Have you ever wondered why we find so little time to pray? And when we do take time, why is it often an unsatisfactory experience? What is prayer, really? Why do we resist its power? We join Jesus' disciples in expressing our need: "Lord, teach us to pray!" Jesus' answer in Luke 11 was first to give us a model prayer. He then told a humorous parable.

Jesus used humor to make a point more than once. Laughter is good preparation for a confrontation with truth. Will Rogers once said that everything is funny as long as it's happening to somebody else. Jesus goes way beyond that. He uses humor to free us to laugh at ourselves. Then when we are loosened up, He identifies us in the ridiculous incongruity. Don't miss the humor in this story!

Picture a Palestinian family having vacated the bottom floor of their house and retreated to the loft to sleep. The door is tightly bolted with a crossbar, and all is dark and quiet. Then at midnight, when everyone is sleeping soundly, there is a persistent knocking on the heavy wooden door. Who can that be at this hour of the night? Imagine getting out of bed, threading your way through the family members sleeping in the one-room loft, climbing down the ladder and picking your way through the animals you have let in to use the bottom floor of the house as a stable for the night.

At the door stands an old friend from a distant village. He has no place to stay and nothing to eat. You have to invite him in, make a place for him and give him a midnight snack. To refuse to do so would be to create an enemy. But you have no bread in the house. What can you do?

Now you have no choice but to go to your neighbor for help. You know that he and his children are in bed, too. Regardless, you must get bread for your visitor. You go to your neighbor's and pound on the door. No answer. You knock again, louder this time. After a long time, you hear him say, angry and perturbed, "Who's there? What do you want at this hour of the night?"

You tell him you need bread for your visitor. "Don't bother me!" your neighbor shouts. "Can't you see the door is shut and we're trying to get some sleep? What are you trying to do—wake the kids?" But you have no alternative, so you knock again. The cattle and other animals that have been let inside for the night are growing restless. Your neighbor realizes that soon they will wake the whole village. Finally he has no alternative: He gets up wearily and gives you the bread.

We laugh. "Well, what would *you* have done?" Jesus asks.

We reply, chuckling, "Why, of course, we'd have to get up and help our neighbor."

Then, suddenly, Jesus gets into serious conversation with us. If a mere man would respond because of the importunity of his neighbor, would not God, who "will neither slumber nor sleep" (Ps. 121:4) answer our prayers? Now we see that Jesus' humorous story has shown us the utter availability of a gracious, loving Father. At any hour of the day or night, He will hear our concerns and meet our needs.

The warm humor of the parable has prepared us for further illustrations that touch our hearts. Would a father give a hungry son a snake instead of a fish, or a scorpion instead of an egg? Everything tender and humane in us recoils. "Of course not, Jesus!" Our emotions are raw from these illustrations. And that's just what Jesus wanted—fertile soil for planting one last truth:

"If you then, being evil, know how to give good gifts to your children, *how much more* shall your heavenly Father give the Holy Spirit to those who ask Him?" (Luke 11:13, italics added).

Kingdom Thinking

1. Do you have the sort of prayer life that can be described as regular, occasional or almost never?

2. Do you have any particular difficulties or recurring problems with prayer? Does God at times seem not to answer?

3. What are the greatest gifts we can receive from prayer? Name six of them. Now rank them in order of their importance.

4. What does prayer assume about the nature of God?

Related Readings

Psalm 61 Matthew 7:7-12 2 Corinthians 13:7-10

Prayer to the King

King of heaven, we praise You for listening to us and caring about what concerns us! Help us to recall the times when You provide our needs even before we ask, instead of remembering only the times we could not perceive Your answer to our prayers. Through Jesus Christ our Lord, Amen.

6

The Available King

Scripture Reading:

There was in a certain city a judge who did not fear God, and did not respect man. And there was a widow in that city, and she kept coming to him, saying, "Give me legal protection from my opponent." And for a while he was unwilling; but afterward he said to himself, "Even though I do not fear God nor respect man, yet because this widow bothers me, I will give her legal protection, lest by continually coming she wear me out."

Luke 18:2-5

Are there times when you wonder why prayer appears to be a dynamic dialogue for some, while for you it's often a monotonous monologue, as if no one were listening? The parable of the unjust judge is a twin to the parable in the previous chapter. Jesus told both stories in response to questions just like this. And again, in this parable, we are exposed to the humor of Jesus.

We can easily imagine how the dignified judge felt. The woman tracks his steps everywhere. She's at his door in the morning, confronts him in the marketplace, interrupts his conversations with esteemed associates, disrupts his court and is waiting for him when he comes home at night. Her appeal is always the same: "Give me legal protection from my opponent!"

A woman, much less a widow, had few rights at this time period. If the rabbis prayed daily, "I thank Thee God that You did not make me a woman," we can imagine the attitude toward widows. All the more reason that the judge's friends begin to tease him about his inability to get rid of this widow. He is known as a hard, impervious judge, who constantly fortifies his self-image by protesting that he does not fear God or respect any person. But he meets his match in this widow. Some lady! The judge has met a Tugboat Annie or a Ma Kettle. The disciples must have had a good belly laugh over the contradiction between the judge's statement of his authority and his growing fear of the widow's threats.

The parable ends with a question and a statement that the humor has prepared us to hear: "Now shall not God bring about justice for His elect, who cry to Him day and night, and will He delay long over them?" (Luke 18:7).

Once again, Jesus has used the "how much more" of convicting comparison. If a persistent, scrappy widow, who is a dangerous nuisance to a hostile, unrighteous judge, can get him to rule favorably in her case, will not the ultimate Judge of the universe act on behalf of His people with justice and mercy?

This parable and that of the importunate friend in the preceding chapter have been greatly misunderstood as merely teaching the value of persistent prayer. More importantly, Jesus wants us to understand that frenzied rapping on the door of heaven and continually coming to the unrighteous judge are expressions of inadequate prayer. If God is our Father and forgiving Judge, He needs to be told of our need only once. He is the available King, not an unrighteous judge. Repeated prayer is not to remind Him, but to thank Him.

A misunderstanding of prayer underlies the reason we don't spend more time in prayer. We find time to do what we want to do. Naturally we won't spend much time in prayer if we think of God as a reluctant neighbor, or as a judge who is more concerned about our failures and inadequacies than He is about justice. On a human level, we will do anything we can to spend time with a person who loves, accepts and affirms us. This parable teaches us that God, as an available King, longs for us to long to spend time with Him, not just seek quick answers to prayer.

The parable also corrects a frequent misunderstanding about answered prayer. The King is more than available; in His sovereign love and knowledge, He sometimes allows the answer to our prayers to develop so they can eventually be perfected for our good. The waiting can be painful, and the silence heavy. But in our asking and seeking and knocking, the King wants us to move from "I want" to "Lord, what do *You* want?"

When we see God as "much more" than the neighbor or the judge in these two parables, we can envision prayer as so much more than banging down a door that is already open, or convincing a judge who has already ruled in our favor. We will understand what Mother Teresa of Calcutta said: "Prayer enlarges the heart until it is capable of containing God's gift of Himself."

Kingdom Thinking

1. Can you think of particular instances when you experienced delayed answers to prayer, only to discover later that it was to your advantage for God not to answer immediately?

2. If God knows everything, why pray? Why has He created us to pray? What are the results of a consistent quiet time of listening prayer? How does that change how we pray?

3. What kinds of prayer do you think God will not answer (see James 1:6,7; 4:3)?

Related Readings

Job 6:8-10 Matthew 6:9-13 James 5:13-18

Prayer to the King

Help us to long for You, more than for what You can do for us, O God. We ascribe to You both the power to grant our every wish, and the knowledge to know when we should not be granted all that we ask for. We believe; help Thou our unbelief. In Jesus' name, Amen.

7

Prayer that Goes Unheard

SCRIPTURE READING:

Two men went up into the temple to pray, one a Pharisee, and the other a tax-gatherer. The Pharisee stood and was praying thus to himself, "God, I thank Thee that I am not like other people: swindlers, unjust, adulterers, or even like this tax-gatherer. I fast twice a week; I pay tithes of all I get."...For everyone who exalts himself shall be humbled, but he who humbles himself shall be exalted.

LUKE 18:10-12,14

I have a friend who claims he has discovered the hidden power of meditation. He takes time each day to be quiet, to gather strength for the challenges and opportunities of each day. During his meditation, he refortifies his belief in himself and in his gifts to win in life's battles. He gives himself ego-boosting affirmations: "You're okay. You can make it. Nothing is too great for you to conquer if you believe in yourself!" My friend asserts that all this is a form of prayer, and that it gives him great confidence and courage.

We smile. That's not prayer! The man is talking to himself, not God. Exactly. But does this man's meditation exemplify the praying of many of us? Much of what we call prayer is little more than a dialogue with ourselves.

Although God can answer all prayers, He does not hear those that are not addressed to Him. It's possible to think we are praying, when all we are doing is refortifying our presuppositions and ruminating within the cycle of our ego-obscured perception of reality. We can even address God with familiar titles of the deity, repeating shibboleths of tattered phrases; but the result is the same: a pious conversation with ourselves!

Jesus told this parable for the express purpose of alarming and helping "certain ones who trusted in themselves that they were righteous, and viewed others with contempt" (Luke 18:9). Who of us can evade the broad sweep of that convicting net of truth? Although "praying to himself" might simply mean praying inaudibly, I think Jesus meant more than that.

The nature of the man's prayer indicates that it was confined to his closed inner chamber of self-sufficiency. This respected religious leader has given us a model not of prayer but of pride. It is that kind of prayer toward which the King of heaven is deaf.

God does not hear the comparative prayer. The Pharisee took the wrong measurements, comparing himself with the tax collector. He was looking down on another human being rather than up to God. He grasped an opportunity to lift himself up by putting another down. But our status with God is not based on being better than others. We are to be all that God has gifted us to be. God has given us the only acceptable basis of comparison: Jesus Christ.

God does not hear the prayer that is based merely on externals. The Pharisee's prayer was built on the unstable foundation of *what he had done*, not *what he was*. Both what he did and abstained from doing were on the surface. He had accomplished it all himself. He had no dependence on God for his impeccable life.

Jesus wants us to understand how pride twists and distorts our capacity for self-scrutiny. Our minds were meant to be truth-gathering computers. But prayers such as that of the Pharisee make us ignore reality and forget things that are beneath the surface agenda of our conscious perceptions. Prayers such as this delude us into thinking that we can be right with God because of our own accomplishments and goodness. They trick us into seeing what we want to see, whether it's true or not. Our minds rationalize to protect our egos. We resist the need to change and grow by identifying our brand of righteousness with God's.

That's why some of our supposed prayers never reach God. The purpose of prayer is to see things as they are: ourselves as we really are, and God as He has revealed Himself to be. God wants us to come to grips with the true person inside us—our hopes and dreams, failures and sins, missed opportunities and potential.

When we can pray without this Pharisaical pride, and are honest with what we want and able to compare it with what God wills for us, the King then hears and answers our prayers.

Kingdom Thinking

1. What are some ways we can avoid "comparative praying," centering our prayers instead on thoughts that God will hear?

2. Tax collectors were the "bad guys" of Jesus' day. Who are some groups that many people instinctively or subconsciously have in mind as unacceptable to God in our time?

3. What are some ways Christians often instinctively or subconsciously present themselves to God as "reasons" why He should look favorably on them?

Related Readings

Proverbs 16:18 Jeremiah 48:40-42 James 4:6-10

Prayer to the King

Help me, O God, to empty myself of my self, so I may be filled with You. Grant that I may come to You without pretense or pride, knowing that You look upon the heart, and that nothing is hidden before You. I confess that even my ability to come before You is not because of my own righteousness, but because of the work of Christ, in whose name I pray, Amen

8

The Servant with an Attitude

SCRIPTURE READING:

But the tax-gatherer, standing some distance away, was even unwilling to lift up his eyes to heaven, but was beating his breast, saying, "God, be merciful to me, the sinner!" I tell you, this man went down to his house justified rather than the other.

LUKE 18:13,14

The pride of the Pharisee in this parable was based on his lack of perceived need for God. He was so righteous he had no need for God, so God had no need for his fictitious prayers.

But the tax collector's prayer is a startling contrast. He desperately needed God. Note his description of himself not as "a" sinner but "*the*" sinner. He saw himself as the greatest of sinners—and probably for good reason. Because tax gatherers were permitted by Rome to keep anything they could squeeze out of people, they were infamous for collecting the required tax plus more for themselves. Jesus did not exonerate the publican for this practice by accepting his prayer. What He did do was expose the taproot of true prayer: the need for God.

What brought the publican to the point where he saw himself as *the* sinner? What brought him so low that he could rise to the sublime heights of prayer? We do not know. But we can imagine, based on our own experience. Life has a way of leveling the growth of proud self-satisfaction. Its tragedies and crises can suddenly diminish the resources of self-sufficiency. It is a special gift of God when we are forced to admit that we can't make it on our own.

But does this mean we have to confess that we are sinners, and especially *the* sinner? Don't we ever outgrow this state of contrition? Even if we admit that we are sinners, aren't we saved by grace? Isn't that what Christianity is all about? Must we hit bottom again and again to be able to pray humbly? And aren't there things we can do to clean up our act so that we have something to show God as the fruit of our humility?

To ask such questions is to indicate a misunderstanding of sin. It is not only separation from God, but also from His purpose and potential for us. We never outgrow our need for God's love, forgiveness, guidance and indwelling power. Assurance of grace initiates aspiration to continue to grow. God is not finished with us; therefore, we are never finished.

As I write this, I am aware of areas in my life and relationships where I need God desperately. My opportunities, not just my failures, drive me back to Him constantly. And right at this moment, as you are reading this, are you not conscious of things said or unsaid, done or left undone, that jab at your conscience? Who can live any day without a disturbing sense of missed opportunities as well as overt sins that have hurt ourselves and others? The apostle Paul called himself the "chief of sinners" (see 1 Tim. 1:15, *KJV*) at a time when he was the leading advocate of the grace of God. He was constantly pressing on in the upward call of Christ Jesus. The closer he got to the Lord, the greater was his need for Him.

It is this ongoing humility that is at stake in the Lord's pronouncement at the end of this parable that it was the tax collector, not the Pharisee, who "went down to his house justified" (Luke 18:14). Pride always leaves us unfulfilled and unsatisfied. Humility opens the floodgates of the heart of God. It is the basic ingredient of any prayer that God will answer.

No one ever achieves humility by seeking it as an end in itself. It is a by-product of something much deeper. Jesus clarified this in the Beatitudes, in His description of true "blessedness" (see Matt. 5:3-12). He showed there that humility is rooted in the fertile soil of spiritual poverty that recognizes our ongoing need for God's power. It grows by a profound grief over what we have done with the gifts of God. It is nurtured by a meekness that longs for His guidance. It is strengthened by mercy (gracious love for others). And it flowers in a dominant desire of the heart to know God, and to do His will at all costs.

None of this implies a hang-dog attitude. The kind of humility that enables us to arise from prayer being justified is actually courageous. Authentic humility is an expression of gratitude, honesty and courage. It asks and answers three crucial questions: What do I have that I was not given? Who am I, really? and, What are the next steps in the adventure of growth for me? Humility is the courage to dare. The Pharisee had no room in his heart for growth. The tax collector's humility made life, and answered prayer, exciting adventures.

Kingdom Thinking

1. Why is honesty about ourselves essential to authentic humility? How can we be humble, and still claim our potential as persons?

2. Before Rabbi Zusia died, he said, "When I shall face the celestial tribunal, I shall not be asked why I

was not Abraham, Jacob or Moses. I shall be asked why I was not Zusia." Is this true or false humility?

3. What is the difference between traits such as healthy self-esteem or "taking pride in our work," and the kind of pride exhibited by the Pharisee in Luke 18:11,12?

4. What is the difference between the kind of humility commended by the Lord in this parable and "false humility"?

Related Readings

2 Chronicles 7:12-14 Psalm 51:14-17
Matthew 23:8-12

Prayer to the King

Great King of heaven, we have only to think of Your glory to realize our unworthiness. Yet, even in our humility we pray for boldness to accept Your promise that You will hear the prayers of the humble, not turning us away even though we have nothing of our own righteousness to bring before Your throne. Through Christ our Lord, Amen.

9

The Heart of Forgiveness

SCRIPTURE READING:

The kingdom of heaven may be compared to a certain king who wished to settle accounts with his slaves. And when he had begun to settle them, there was brought to him one who owed him ten thousand talents....And the lord of that slave felt compassion and released him and forgave him the debt.

MATTHEW 18:23,24,27

At the heart of the Kingdom of heaven is the King's heart of forgiveness. The parable of the unmerciful servant was given in response to a blush of magnanimity by Simon Peter. He thought he could impress the Master with his benevolent offer: "Lord, how often shall my brother sin against me and I forgive him?" Simon set himself up for his own answer: "Up to seven times?" (Matt. 18:21).

The Lord's response was like a dagger. It pierced Simon's puffed-up piety when Jesus used a Hebraism for infinity. "Seventy times seven" meant without limits. Why? Because that is the astounding capacity of the King's forgiveness, and we are to be to others what He has been to us.

To illustrate, Jesus tells of a king who wanted to settle his accounts with his debtors. One of them owed him ten thousand talents. A talent was worth about a thousand dollars. Simple arithmetic captures our attention. Ten million dollars! Quite a debt. We are amazed. When the debtor could not pay, the king followed the law of the land: the debtor, his wife and children were sentenced to be sold into slavery.

Then we are surprised to learn that when the man prostrated himself before the king, asking for time so he could repay the debt, the king felt compassion, released the man and forgave the debt. What kind of king is this? Jesus had a greater King than any human potentate in mind: God. The immensity of the debt is forgiven by the immutable love of the King of Creation. The servant felt the heartbeat of forgiveness—the center and core of how the Kingdom operates.

We shall consider in the next chapter the role in

which we are cast in this drama—that of the servant. For the moment, we note that the lighting of the scene casts an odd shadow across the stage. It's a cross! We must interpret the parable from this side of calvary. "Paid in full" is written across all our sins and debts.

This is a new rendition of *The King and I*. How shall we respond to the King when He calls us to account for our debt? We can have no other posture than on our knees, begging for mercy. Amazing grace! It's been extended in spite of all we've said and done. We are free because the polluted waters of our soul have been purified with a red substance flowing freely. The blood of the Lamb! Can we ever deserve a love like that? No!

The fact is, we are in debt to God. Paul was right: "All have sinned and fall short of the glory of God" (Rom. 3:23). Our sin is rebellion against God: the willful desire to run our own lives, to shape our own destiny, to live by our own strength and grit. Our sins flow from the headwaters of that separation. How can we repay the debt we owe for the ravage we make of our lives, the lives of others and of the creation entrusted to us? We can't. No more than the unmerciful servant could raise ten million dollars to pay the king. All we can do is ask for mercy and forgiveness.

And lo! the King responds to our plea. He sends His only Son, Jesus, to save His people from their sins. The cost was high! Calvary. It was there that Psalm 130 was enacted: "If Thou, Lord, shouldst mark iniquities, O Lord, who could stand? But there is forgiveness with Thee, that Thou mayest be feared....For with the Lord there is lovingkindness, and with Him is abundant redemption" (vv. 3,4,7).

Or consider Psalm 103: "As far as the east is from the west, so far has He removed our transgressions from us. Just as a father has compassion on his children, so the Lord has compassion on those who fear Him" (vv. 12,13). And Isaiah peered into the future to the Cross when he wrote: "Though your sins are as scarlet, they will be as white as snow; though they are red like crimson, they will be like wool" (Isa. 1:18).

Nothing we could ever do could earn the Cross. But this parable does tell us something we can do *in response* to the Cross. That response, which is also at the heart of the kingdom of God, will be considered in the next chapter.

Kingdom Thinking

1. Romans 5:8 says, "God demonstrates His own love toward us, in that while we were yet sinners, Christ died for us." Does God provide the means of our forgiveness before or after we confess our sins? How about after we become Christians? What does this say about our attitude to people who have hurt or harmed us?

2. What human characteristic lies behind Peter's feeling that he was being more than gracious in sug-

gesting that he might be able to forgive a person "seven times"?

3. If the figure "ten thousand talents" represents a sum no ordinary person could ever repay, what does the parable imply about the number or the magnitude of the various sins God will forgive?

Related Readings

Psalm 103:8-10 Isaiah 53:3-6 Romans 3:23-28

Prayer to the King

Praise be to You, our Father, for the unspeakable gift of Jesus Christ Your Son and our Savior! Without having seen Him, we love Him; for without our having earned His favor, He first loved us. Grant that we might now live in the confidence and power that befit forgiven people. Through Jesus we pray, Amen.

10

What Comes Around Must Go Around

SCRIPTURE READING:

But that slave went out and found one of his fellow slaves who owed him a hundred denarii; and he seized him and began to choke him, saying "Pay back what you owe." Then summoning him, his lord said to him, "You wicked slave, I forgave you all that debt because you entreated me. Should you not also have had mercy on your fellow slave?"

MATTHEW 18:28,32,33

We think of God as "omniscient" or all powerful, and He is. But one thing He will not do. The parable of the unmerciful servant tells us that God will not forgive us if we do not forgive others. The parable stabs us awake by the discrepancy between the ten million dollars the king forgave his servant, and the measly hundred denarii—perhaps twenty dollars—the man's fellow servant owed him. Our surprise turns to anger and then to rage over the debtor's behavior. After all the king had done for him, how could he have so little compassion for one who owed such a paltry amount?

It's difficult to imagine the servant's pitiless attitude and actions. He took his debtor by the throat, throttling and choking him—which was permitted in Roman law. Then he threw the twenty-dollar debtor into prison. It was his right! But how could he do it after all the mercy he had received?

The king asks the same question. Outraged, he revokes the forgiveness he had extended to his servant in the first place. "Should you not also have had mercy on your fellow slave, even as I had mercy on you?" asks the king (Matt. 18:33). In anger, the king hands over his servant to the torturers "until he should repay all that was owed him" (v. 34). Then, the story ended, Jesus looks at us and drives home the point of the parable: "So shall My heavenly Father also do to you, if each of you does not forgive his brother from your heart" (v. 35).

Why? Because the Kingdom of heaven is to perpetuate itself by people who respond to others with the grace that the King has extended to them. After telling us in the parable about the behavior of God, Jesus then confronts us with whether or not we are willing to behave toward others in such a manner. What came around to us must now go around to others.

Forgiving others "from your heart" is a burred hook. We can't slip off by saying we will forgive but not forget. Or that we will forgive the person, but not the deed. Cheap forgiveness! Verbalism without a vital, reconciled relationship. All such measures are ways of trying to evade the responsibility of reproducing in our own lives the awesome completeness of God's forgiveness of us.

Although we can never deserve the kind of love God extends to us, this parable shows that we can negate it. What has happened since we were born again and received new life? That's the aching question of the parable. Has it made any difference? Have we forgiven as we've been forgiven? Has our attitude to people around us been consistent with God's acceptance of us?

John Wesley once heard a man say, "I never forgive." His response was incisive: "Then I hope, sir, that you never sin." Indeed. Our forgiveness from God is intertwined inseparably with our willingness to forgive. The principle is so crucial that Jesus made it a central tenet of the disciple's prayer: "Forgive us our debts, as we also have forgiven our debtors" (Matt. 6:12). And in the Beatitudes He said, "Blessed are the merciful, for they shall receive mercy" (Matt. 5:7).

A woman once came up to me after a class on this topic, having tears stream down her face. "This morning I realized that I have to forgive my mother!" she said. Then followed a painful account of what her mother had done to her in her childhood. The woman's resentment seemed more than justified on the human level. But hatred festered in her soul. She had wondered often why she could not experience the joy of God's grace. That morning she discovered the reason: She had not forgiven her mother. The Holy Spirit had taken the words of this parable and pierced her unforgiving spirit.

Yet, I am amazed at how few church members understand this principle. Recently I made a survey of Bible-believing Christians to ascertain how many remembered or understood Matthew 18:35. Only *one out of ten* even knew it was in the New Testament! No wonder we find Paul's words to the Ephesians so difficult: "Be kind to one another, tender-hearted, forgiving each other, just as God in Christ also has forgiven you" (Eph. 4:32).

Kingdom Thinking

1. Take the time to make a list of the things for which God has forgiven you, thanking Him for His grace.
2. Now make a list of those who have hurt you,

whom you have not fully forgiven. Imagine the forgiveness you experienced when thinking of the first list being revoked because of your attitudes toward those on the second list. Are your grudges or feelings of ill will really worth it?

3. Ask God for the grace of forgiveness toward others, releasing each person on your second list to Him.

4. Depending on the situation, speak or write notes to those toward whom you have a fresh, forgiving spirit.

Related Readings

Matthew 7:1-5 Luke 7:40-47 Romans 12:17-21

Prayer to the King

Dear Father, help me to extend to others the grace You have extended to me. Grant me freedom from grudges and resentments over hurts in the past, and from double standards that require more of others than of myself. In the name of Jesus who has forgiven me, Amen.

11

Elected by Love

SCRIPTURE READING:

For the kingdom of heaven is like a landowner who went out early in the morning to hire laborers for his vineyard. And when he had agreed with the laborers for a denarius for the day, he sent them into his vineyard. And he went out about the third hour and...about the sixth and the ninth hour,...and about the eleventh hour...and found others...and he said to them, "You too go into the vineyard."

MATTHEW 20:1-7

The parable of the laborers in the vineyard stuns us. What did Jesus imply by calling workers at different times during the day, only to pay them all the same amount? Can we accept this seeming inequality about God's administration of the Kingdom? Whatever happened to the idea that long, hard labor and faithfulness have their reward?

The parable had been motivated by the Lord's discussion with the disciples about the reward of following Him. Peter, like the full-day laborer, wanted to negotiate for some assurance that the cost of following the Master would be worth it all. "Behold, we have left everything and followed You; what then will there be for us?" (Matt. 19:27). Jesus' response is very direct: "Truly I say to you, that you who have followed Me, in the regeneration when the Son of Man will sit on His glorious throne, you also shall sit upon twelve thrones, judging the twelve tribes of Israel. And everyone who has left houses or brothers or sisters or father or mother or children or farms for My name's sake, shall receive many times as much, and shall inherit eternal life" (vv. 28,29).

The question of all the workers being paid the same, regardless of how long they labored in the vineyard, will be addressed in the next chapter. For now, dwell on the glory of grace—of being called at all. The only basis of any hope at all is that God has elected us to know Him, to receive His love, to experience salvation through Christ's death and resurrection, and to enjoy the delight of His indwelling Spirit. We did nothing to deserve it or earn it. Our calling is a gift.

Paul captured this magnificent truth. "And we know that God causes all things to work together for good to those who love God, to those who are called according to His purpose. For whom He foreknew, He also predestined to become conformed to the image of His Son, that He might be the first-born among many brethren; and whom He predestined, these He also called; and whom He called, these He also justified; and whom He justified, these He also glorified" (Rom. 8:28-30).

Many of our questions about the equity of the pay meted out to the laborers in the vineyard will evaporate if we dwell sufficiently on the grace of being elected by love. We did not choose Christ; He chose us. Long before our desire to respond to His love, He was at work in us, creating in us the longing for Him to fill our emptiness. We are in His vineyard, early or late, by sheer grace. And if we deserve absolutely no credit because we are there, how can we have envy or jealousy about the payment received by others?

I recently had the privilege of introducing an old man and a teenage woman to Christ. A sixteen-year-old woman named Beth was filled with the joy and peace of Christ, and with excitement about a full life ahead, a life of growing in the Savior. She entered the vineyard early.

The elderly man was close to the end of his life. His energies are spent; all he had to bring to the Lord was a long life of regrets. His whole life had been spent on himself and his own desires. The plow of self-concern had cut deep furrows on his brow and lines in his face. Now sickness had brought him to the realization of his desperate need for God. He was not ready to die. He feared the judgment of God. As he repeated the sinner's prayer after me, I sensed the presence of the loving Lord. Afterward he said, "How I wish I hadn't waited so long. There's not much time left to enjoy my new life." I assured him he had all of eternity.

Can you imagine the young woman resenting that? Far from being jealous, it is more likely that she would pity the elderly man for his lost years, and rejoice in the grace extended to her early in life. The fact is, neither had earned the gracious gift of salvation. One early, one late. Both were elected by love. Isn't that enough?

Kingdom Thinking

1. In his book *In Quest of a Kingdom*, Leslie Weatherhead invites us to trace our call into God's vineyard by correlating a life of seventy years with the waking hours of a single day, from 7:00 A.M. until 11:00 P.M.

If you are age 15, the time is 10:25 A.M.

Age	20	=	11:34 A.M.
	25	=	12:42 P.M.
	30	=	1:51 P.M.
	35	=	3:00 P.M.

40	=	4:08 P.M.
45	=	5:16 P.M.
50	=	6:25 P.M.
55	=	7:34 P.M.
60	=	8:42 P.M.
65	=	9:51 P.M.
70	=	11:00 P.M.[1]

2. Reflect on the time of your own calling, and how long you may have until the Master of the vineyard presents you with your wages. Place the emphasis not on regrets for lost time, but on rejoicing that you have been elected by love.

Related Readings

Isaiah 65:8-10 Romans 9:21-26 1 Corinthians 15:8-11

Prayer to the King

We confess that the mystery of Your grace is above our ways, O Lord, and that Your thoughts are above our thoughts. Grant that we may respond to having been called into Your kingdom by living up to our calling. Through Jesus Christ our Lord, Amen.

Note

1. Leslie D. Weatherhead, *In Quest of a Kingdom* (Nashville, TN: Abingdon-Cokesbury Press, n.d.), p. 138.

12

The Reward of His Presence

SCRIPTURE READING:

And when evening had come, the owner of the vineyard said to his foreman, "Call the laborers and pay them their wages, beginning with the last group to the first." And when those hired first came, they thought that they would receive more; and they also received each one a denarius. And when they received it, they grumbled at the landowner, saying, "These last men have worked only one hour, and you have made them equal to us who have borne the burden and the scorching heat of the day."

MATTHEW 20:8,10-12

The sirocco woke the man from a deep sleep. He could hear the desert winds relentlessly blowing the trees outside and whistling through the cracks and crevices of his house. It was the time of scorching heat. The grapes would have to be harvested! He dressed quickly and hurried to the marketplace where day laborers waited each day for work. The negotiations with the owner of the vineyard went quickly: A denarius was offered, and the laborers agreed.

The early morning hours in the vineyard were usually cool and motivated energetic work. Not that day. Even the early sun was blisteringly hot, and the winds felt as if they had been blown off a furnace. The laborer began his garnering with skilled hands, trained by years of hard labor. But as he looked over the vineyard and all the grapes to be harvested, he knew that the early morning crew the owner had hired would not be able to finish before sundown.

At nine in the morning the owner returned to the marketplace to see if any more laborers could be hired. *It would be good to have help*, the man thought. In his mind, he speculated what the latecomers would be paid in comparison with the denarius that was a full day's wage. Again and again the owner brought more laborers—right on up to 5:00 P.M., almost time to quit. Would they be satisfied with only one-twelfth of a denarius? Or would the owner pay those who had started early even more than they had agreed on?

Finally, the grapes are harvested, and the workers line up for their pay. The man is amazed when the laborers who had not been hired until 5:00 P.M. receive a denarius. How can this be? Perhaps the master of the vineyard will pay him all the more. Then anger surges through him as the foreman places in his hand the same amount—a single denarius for twelve hours' work—no more than the men who worked only one hour!

As we noticed in the preceding chapter, this parable is mainly about God's unmerited love. We are elected by love. This is a source of amazement for some and alarm for others. There are people who find it difficult to believe that God loves them in spite of what they have been or done. Others find it an affront that God does not love them *because* of what they've been or done. But Jesus is very clear in the parable: The wage is the same for all.

But what a wage! Instead of dwelling on the size of the coin in the parable, enlarge the point of the story to the size of the gift of God's grace. Those who enter the kingdom of God are given eternal life—abundant life now and forever! The important thing is not when we come into the vineyard, but that, having come early or late, we are all brought into the presence of the owner of the vineyard.

Think of it! Companionship is our compensation. To labor with the Lord, long or short, is the blessing that is ours by grace. A sixteenth-century prayer articulates this joy. "Teach us to labor and not to ask for any reward save that of knowing that we do Thy will." Thomas Aquinas knew the essence of that. Once he heard the Lord say to him in a dream, "Thomas, thou hast written much and well concerning Me. What reward shall I give thee for thy work?" Thomas's reply was, "Nothing but Thyself, Lord!" Companionship with the Lord is the ultimate reward. We are free to love God for Himself, not because of what He will do for us or because of what we have done for Him.

I heard one of the elders of our church pray, "Thank You, Lord, that You called me on my mother's knee and helped me to know You as a child so that I could enjoy You all through the years." If you can say that, praise God. But if it's the noon hour of your life, the invitation is open. And if it's the last hour, it's not too late. A companionship that death cannot end can begin right now.

Kingdom Thinking

1. What is the difference between *wages earned* and the reward for working in God's vineyard (see Rom. 4:4,5)?

2. What is the difference between paying an hourly wage to workers, and the reward God gives workers in His vineyard? (Could God pay latecomers into His

vineyard a *fraction* of eternal life?) What are the six most important things we receive when we live and work for God as the King of our lives?

3. What does this parable have to say to people who are traditionally religious, but have not experienced the new birth?

4. How do you feel about stories of "death-bed conversions"?

Related Readings

Psalm 16:7-11 John 10:14-16 Revelation 22:1-5

Prayer to the King

Dear Lord, in my better moments I am glad to leave the salvation of others to Your goodness and grace. Help me to be satisfied with living in Your presence, both here and hereafter. In the name of Jesus I pray, Amen.

13

Who Owns This Vineyard?

SCRIPTURE READING:

There was a landowner who planted a vineyard and put a wall around it and dug a wine press in it, and built a tower, and rented it out to vine-growers, and went on a journey. And when the harvest time approached, he sent his slaves....afterward he sent his son to them, saying, "They will respect my son." But when the vine-growers saw the son, they said among themselves, "This is the heir; come, let us kill him, and seize his inheritance."

MATTHEW 21:33,34,37,38

The vinedressers loved to stand in the tower and survey their work. They were proud of the healthy vines, row upon row, neatly cultivated and cared for. They could boast of having worked arduously under the sweltering sun, trimming, pruning, fertilizing. The hedge protecting the vineyard was a mason's masterpiece, stone upon stone. The wine vat for pressing the wine from the grapes had been carefully excavated, one part being a bit higher than the other so the lower portion could receive the flow of new wine from the ripened grapes.

The owner of the vineyard had been gone so long that the vinedressers had begun to think of the vineyard as their own. *After all, there would be no harvest without us*, they thought. Indignation and resentment surged through them as they reflected on the terms of the lease, which called for them to return to the landowner one-third of the profits. A third! It's not fair!

One day, from their position atop the tower, the vinedressers saw three distant figures making their way toward the vineyard through the mountain pass. The landowner's servants! The vinedressers knew what they wanted. The servants had come to collect the landowner's profit. Anger and greed arose in them like a tide. They beat one servant, killed another and stoned the third servant senseless.

The next year at about the same time, another group of slaves approached the vineyard. They met the same fate. In the third year, watchmen in the tower saw a solitary figure coming through the pass. As he drew near, they could see his resemblance to the owner of the vineyard. It was his son! If they did away with him, the vineyard would be theirs by simple right of possession, would it not? In a final act of both murder and theft, they slew the son. The vineyard was theirs.

Or was it? Israel was the vineyard of the Lord. The prophets had come to claim His ownership and the fruit of righteousness from His tremendous investment. But Israel's leaders had slain the prophets, resenting anyone who threatened their authority over the people. Now they are threatening the rabbi from Nazareth who had entered *their* city and challenged their practices.

But there is more to the story. Return with me to the tower. What is the vineyard for us? Our life, plans, future? It may be a loved one, our family, anyone whom we force to be an extension of our own ego. Our image, our career, our church. Investments, trophies of success, properties. The images shift, but the message is the same.

We begin to act as if the vineyard is our own. We earned it, didn't we? We want no one, not even God, to menace our self-management. We have rejected repeated overtures to acknowledge His ownership of our lives, "killing off" or banishing the voices who would remind us that the vineyard is only leased out to us. And even the Son—how often has He come to claim what is His, only to be rejected, stoned and beaten in our ecclesiastical structures, neglected in our culturalized religion, domesticated in our irrelevant piety?

When did the transition from His to ours to mine take place for you? It happens before we know it. Gradually, we neglect to read the owner's manual telling us how to manage the vineyard. Our arduous labor, we believe, gives us right of ownership. We may be willing to acknowledge that the landowner created the vineyard, but surely He did it for us, and we have made it what it is by effort and tireless striving. We leaf through our checkbooks and our investment of time and energy and recoil at the idea of returning even a tenth to the landowner, much less a third! Gradually, we don't even think of the landowner except in times of crisis, when our vines yield no grapes.

There is a better way, one that will occupy our attention in the next chapter. For now, let us not soften the accusing tone of this parable. Let us acknowledge how easy it is for us to assume that we own this vineyard!

Kingdom Thinking

1. Recall an instance from the Old Testament that Jesus may have had in mind when He told of the landowner's servants (the prophets) being rejected by the vinedressers (Israel's leaders).

2. What steps can be taken to defend against the assumption that we are not mere stewards, but that who we are and what we have are the products of our own efforts?

3. Suppose you have your own business. Give a specific example of the kind of practice this parable warns against. How does this apply to our possessions, plans and the people we love? What is the source of the idea that we own what we have? How can we overcome this?

Related Readings

Psalm 50:7-15 Luke 17:7-10 James 4:13-17

Prayer to the King

All that we have and all that we are come from Your hand, O Lord. Forgive us when we act as though they are possessions of our own making, when we hoard our gifts for ourselves, and when we refuse to acknowledge that every good and perfect gift comes from You. In Jesus' name, Amen.

14

Under New Management

SCRIPTURE READING:

Therefore when the owner of the vineyard comes, what will he do to those vine-growers? They said to Him, "He will bring those wretches to a wretched end, and will rent out the vineyard to other vine-growers, who will pay him the proceeds at the proper seasons."

MATTHEW 21:40,41

As we noted in the preceding chapter, Israel's leaders refused to acknowledge that God's vineyard was not their private possession. They even killed the Son. But look! Yet another figure is coming through the pass toward the vineyard. As he draws near, we again recognize the vineyard Owner's Son—although this time we see nail prints in His hands and a wound in His side. But He is back—risen from the dead! The ultimate point of the parable of the landowner is that we can acknowledge God's ownership over the vineyard of our lives through accepting Christ as Savior and Lord. He will forgive every failure, sin or arrogant demand to run the vineyard if we acknowledge that it is under new ownership!

How can we keep the ownership of our lives where it rightfully belongs? First, by acknowledging the preeminent privilege of life itself. Breathe your next breath with awe and wonder. Feel your pulse. Think with your mind. Sense the emotions you can express. We have been wondrously made to express the love of God. Just as the owner of the vineyard left all the resources to the vinedressers, so God has equipped us to live fully and joyously.

Second, think about the abundant allocation. The Lord has woven all our challenges and opportunities to create the person He has meant us to be. He is the playwright of our experiences, the director of our affairs, the stage manager of our circumstances—all that we might praise Him and live our lives to His glory.

Third, evaluate the tragic transition when we claim the vineyard as our own. It has happened to all of us, this tendency to allow the word "my" to take on dangerous proportions. We start out working for the Lord, and then we want the Lord to work for us. Soon He is dealt out of any partnership in the development of our lives. But because He is in search of people who humbly acknowledge Him as the owner of the vineyard, we soon run out of power on our own. Tragically, the vineyard falls into disrepair and unfruitfulness.

Fourth, be aware of the justice of the judgment pronounced by the owner of the vineyard. A clergyman in the midwest lost his church as the result of a tragic moral indiscretion. I will never forget what he said to me: "I ran my life and my church as if they belonged to me. I felt above checking and accountability. Then it happened. I did something I never thought I would do. Now I've lost everything."

A father told me of having treated his son as his own private possession, demanding performance and perfection he had never been able to accomplish with his own life. Finally, the boy left home and avoided all contact. The father's face had a pitiful look when he said, "I've lost my boy."

A young wife told me that her husband was suing for divorce. Although she didn't believe in divorce, she was having to face up to what she had done to cause the fractured relationship. "There was a moment when I could have changed," she said, "but I couldn't, or I guess I mean that I wouldn't. My husband needed warmth and all he got was control and stiff-armed rejection from me. Now it's too late." She had treated the marriage as her own possession, instead of a trust to be tended to and cherished.

A fifth aspect emerges from this parable as we consider it from this side of the Resurrection. Pentecost and Easter are the reason we see the Son coming again to the vineyard. The same God who judges us for grasping at possession of the vineyard sends His Son again in love. The living Lord returns to the vineyard of our lives. Now the grace of calvary enables us to accept His ownership of the vineyard. We have a new opportunity to invite Him in and say, "Lord, this is your vineyard. It's never belonged to me even though I've acted as if it did. Forgive me. Thank you for your persistence and all your overtures of love, even though I rejected them."

And the Son's response is firm and gracious: "You belong to me. Let us enjoy the vineyard together!"

Kingdom Thinking

1. Recall from your own experience or observation an example of a person who has been able to achieve success while confessing that God has ownership over his or her life.

2. Do people sometimes try to assume unrightful control, even over their religious lives (see 1 Sam. 15:17-23)?

3. How can someone who has acted as though he or she owned the vineyard, and then experienced difficulties or tragedies as a result, regain a sense of joy in the Lord?

Related Readings

Genesis 1:26-31 Psalm 100 Isaiah 2:5-11

Prayer to the King

For our attempts to be masters of our own lives, we pray Your forgiveness, O Lord. We confess that Yours is the vineyard, Yours are the fruits of our labors, Yours is the power and glory forever and ever, Amen.

15

Knowing What We Want, Wanting What We Know

SCRIPTURE READING:

To what then shall I compare the men of this generation, and what are they like? They are like children who sit in the market place and call to one another; and they say, "We played the flute for you, and you did not dance; we sang a dirge, and you did not weep." For John the Baptist has come eating no bread and drinking no wine; and you say, "He has a demon!" The Son of Man has come eating and drinking; and you say, "Behold a gluttonous man, and a drunkard, a friend of tax-gatherers and sinners!"

LUKE 7:31-34

What would you say is the purpose of your life? How would you define your ultimate purpose and your unique, personal purpose? When either our ultimate or our unique purpose becomes clouded or confused, we find that we lose an essential quality of life: earnestness. Earnestness is distinguished by deep feeling, conviction, resoluteness and dedication. When we lose earnestness, we are no longer direct, zealous or fervent.

That's what had happened to the Pharisees. As Luke 7:30 tells us, they had rejected God's call to repentance and renewal by rejecting John the Baptist. In response to this critical spiritual sickness, Jesus told the parable of the children at play in the marketplace. And don't forget that the Pharisees were the religious leaders of the time. What happened to them can happen to us. We can get just enough religion to make us rigid, but lose the purpose that releases power.

Every one of Jesus' listeners had observed children restlessly trying to find a game to play on a long, hot afternoon. Some wanted to play "weddings" and others wanted to play "funerals." The division of desires separated the group in the marketplace. They taunted each other with pique and petulance. One group cried, "We wanted to play wedding, and you wouldn't play our game!" The others replied, "But we wanted to play funeral and you wouldn't do what we wanted." The children didn't know what they wanted, and they ended up enjoying neither game.

The parable of the children at play was Jesus' dramatic characterization of the leaders of Israel who rejected the purpose of God. They didn't like John because he was too ascetic; they didn't like Jesus because of His hearty affirmation of life. John was written off as one who had a demon; Jesus was not taken seriously because He ate with tax collectors and sinners. John was too serious, Jesus not serious enough. They played one off against the other. They neither knew what they wanted nor wanted what they knew.

We are part of the drama that is staged in this parable. Jesus came. What have we done with the truth of His message and the gift of His forgiving death? No one can read this parable seriously without asking, What would I have done with Jesus of Nazareth? Our answer depends on what we are doing now.

Our ultimate purpose is Jesus Christ: to know Him, to allow Him to love us, to love Him in response and to love others as He loved us. Each of us is then called to live out that purpose in the unique circumstances and opportunities of our individual lives. Our concern will be to discover and do the will of God in all of life. He will deploy us in situations and with people where we can be effective for Him. We will know what we want: Christ. We will want what we know: His indwelling power.

I talked to a church officer in a midwest church who had drifted from earnestness of purpose to equivocation. He said, "I am sure about what I don't want, but I don't know what I want. I'm against almost everything that's proposed, but I am at a loss to make a positive suggestion for what we should be doing." His situation reminds us that if we don't know where we are going, we will be negative and critical of where others might want to go.

The earnest Lord of all says, "For I know the plans that I have for you,...plans for welfare and not for calamity to give you a future and a hope. Then you will call upon Me and come and pray to Me, and I will listen to you. And you will seek Me and find Me, when you search for Me with all your heart" (Jer. 29:11-13).

A purpose is available that demands an earnestness now and for all eternity. Instead of playing games, we have a game plan for a truly exciting life.

Kingdom Thinking

1. Have you ever formulated a statement of your purpose in life, the way many businesses write a "mission statement"? If not, take the time right now to develop one.

2. As an overall purpose statement, what do you think of this statement from the *Westminster Shorter Catechism*: "Man's chief end is to glorify God and to enjoy Him for ever"?

3. What are some ways to respond to others that are

more constructive than those of the man in the mid-west church?

Related Readings

1 Samuel 3:1-9 John 12:27,28 Philippians 3:7-11

Prayer to the King

Dear Lord, help us to hear Your call and perceive Your purpose for us above all the other voices that clamor for attention in our lives. Deliver us, we pray, from a bland and drifting life. Enable us to focus on what we should do, and to do that on which we focus. In Jesus' dear name we pray, Amen.

Part II

Living in Light of the Kingdom

16

Christians with a Tang

SCRIPTURE READING:

If anyone comes to Me, and does not hate his own father and mother and wife and children and brothers and sisters, yes, and even his own life, he cannot be My disciple....Salt is good; but if even salt has become tasteless, with what will it be seasoned? It is useless either for the soil or for the manure pile; it is thrown out. He who has ears to hear, let him hear.

LUKE 14:26,34,35

Luke 14:25-35 is a compilation of several parables that describe how Christians can experience the joy of abundant living. And, like skipping over to the end of a novel to see how it comes out, the passage needs to be interpreted from the bottom up. When we do this, we see that Jesus uses all these parables to describe Christians who have a tang—distinctive, sharp, pungent. Salty Christians who have an incisive quality that brings out the flavor of living, seasoning the life of others and society. Saline saints that bring zest and gusto to life.

It should come as no surprise that this remarkable quality of life is costly. Right from the start, Jesus introduces one of the most stringent demands of discipleship: putting Him above family loyalties, and even one's own life. The word "hate" is comparative, meaning in comparison to our love for Christ. Jesus is saying that tangy, zestful Christians are those who allow Him to penetrate their lives so thoroughly that His life in them goes beyond every other loyalty. If we want to become effective, joyful Christians—the salt of the earth—the Lord must pervade to the depths of our being without being tempered by any other commitment.

As every Scot knows, salt must be put into the oatmeal from the start, before cooking, not afterward. In a similar way, Christ can never be added as an afterthought to an already full and committed life. It's possible to attempt to use the Master and His power to fulfill our desires and plans for the people we love and still give Him the one position He will not accept: second place.

The amazing thing about this teaching is that it gives us the key to becoming people who can love themselves and those who are dearest to them with liberating, tangy, in-depth love. Once we love Christ more than ourselves or other people, we are empowered to invest ourselves in creative caring. There's a lively, salty gusto about our love. It's not self-conscious, studied or bartered. An attractive, winsome, lover of people is one who has been liberated from self-consciousness. He can affirm others, build them up, help them to live fully—all because his love is not squandered on the insecurity of self-concern.

How can anyone learn to so love Christ that he can thoroughly love others? Through the power of the Cross: "Whoever does not carry his own cross and come after Me cannot be My disciple" (Luke 14:27). The cross was an instrument of execution. What Jesus meant was that we can be freed to put Him first only if we have crucified our own desires, plans and priorities. Only a cross can put to death the clamor of lesser loves and loyalties.

Seen from this perspective, the cross of Christ is also the basis of the Christian's zesty, passionate concern for others. As forgiven people, we have the salt of forgiveness to heal the wounds of other people. As Christ has seasoned our own lives with forgiveness, we share with others this saving power, showing them Christ's amazing power to purify their distorted lives and setting them free from the bondage of guilt and jaded memories. As the salt of the earth, we can communicate the hope of a new life and a new relationship with God.

When carrying our own cross means death to ourselves and our self-will, we are born again. We are resurrected with Christ for a new life of loving others as He has loved us. The impelling vigor of this is the source of our compassion for and acceptance of others. Our cross even implies a willingness to suffer for people that they may know Christ's love for them.

When our allegiance to Christ empowers us to live in such a way, we will not only be Christians with a tang, but we will also have discovered the true joy of living!

Kingdom Thinking

1. Jesus said, "You are the salt of the earth; but if the salt loses its flavor, how shall it be seasoned?" (Matt. 5:13, *NKJV*). How do Christians lose their tang? How can it be restored? How would you advise a person who wants to regain the zest and gusto of being a Christian?

2. Paul said, "Let your speech always be with grace, seasoned, as it were, with salt, so that you may know how you should respond to each person" (Col. 4:6). In the light of this principle, how do we do this?

3. Is there a risk that those who place Christ first at

the expense of other relationships might become *smug*, instead of just joyful? What is Christ's test of the authentic result of putting Him first?

Related Readings

Psalm 57:7-11 Luke 18:18-23 Luke 18:28-30

Prayer to the King

Dear Lord, help us to see the wisdom of loving You above all loves, and the new life available to us through crucifying our self-centered desires. And, freed from competing loyalties and the insecurity of self-love, help us to love others more generously. Through Jesus we pray, Amen.

17

The Unprepared Disciple

SCRIPTURE READING:

Or what king, when he sets out to meet another king in battle, will not first sit down and take counsel whether he is strong enough with ten thousand men to encounter the one coming against him with twenty thousand? Or else, while the other is still far away, he sends a delegation and asks terms of peace.

LUKE 14:31,32

Jesus continues to illustrate the cost of discipleship in this brief parable as well as in the one preceding: "Which one of you, when he wants to build a tower, does not first sit down and calculate the cost, to see if he has enough to complete it?" (Luke 14:28). All of this is to dramatize a traumatic truth—don't begin discipleship without understanding the high cost of faithfulness. But remember the point at the end of these parables: Jesus is not extracting painful duty from us, but showing us the way to zesty, tangy Christian joy—the abundant life that eludes us when we withhold ourselves from total commitment.

These two parables have a hidden meaning. At first glance, we accept the surface meaning that challenges us to be sure we have what it takes to be a disciple. The deeper meaning of the parables is that, on our own, we will *never* have enough of what it takes. Jesus wants to make clear that what He guides He supplies. Discipleship is not mustering up our own resources, but receiving from our Lord what is required in each new situation and relationship. Christ is doing us a favor by warning us to count the cost. He is saving us from the ridicule we would earn if we were like a man who started a watch tower from which to guard a vineyard, then was not able to complete it (see v. 29), or like a king defeated in a war he launched with insufficient troops.

Consider a king who went into battle unprepared because he did not compare his own army with that of his enemy. A king in battle deals with conflict, just as Jesus came to do battle with the forces of Satan. He called His disciples to be soldiers in that battle. But the Lord wants us to realize that we will lose the battle against evil without Him. A prepared Christian warrior will realize that the gates of hell cannot prevail against him if he calls on the superior forces of the indwelling Lord. The unprepared warrior dashes off into battle on his own resources, and finds them inadequate.

Jesus gives the two alternatives to dependence on His strength: We become immobilized and never get into the battle, or we make peace with an entangling compromise. The point is that Jesus has called us to warfare with evil in people and the structures of society. Such a life will always seem like a battle with ten thousand men against twenty thousand. But this is so that, like Gideon, we can depend on the Lord and not on the size of our own troops. Our amazement will be about what the Lord can do to win the battle for us. We always have a majority when the Lord is on our side.

It is no accident that Jesus adds the saying in verse 33 at this point: "So therefore, no one of you can be My disciple who does not give up all his own possessions." Are we to sell all we have, or is there a more profound meaning in this teaching? I think the Lord meant that we are to give up our right to have and hold life's possessions when they get in the way of immediate and complete allegiance. Applied to the parable of a king going into battle, it means that if we expect to conquer the forces of evil, we must give up the fiction that our own forces are sufficient for the task, and instead call on the power of the Lord through His indwelling Spirit.

Recently, I arrived at church to lead a Sunday evening service and I was completely exhausted. Before the service, I had a deep time of fellowship and prayer with my elders. They discerned the source of the energy drain in worry over an impossible load of detail and uncompleted tasks. I had begun to take the whole responsibility of a new program on myself. When they prayed, laying hands on me, I felt a new freedom to let go of my control, of my own limited and inadequate resources, and to call on the armies of the Lord. After prayer, we all went into the sanctuary to lead a communion and healing service. I felt new energy, enthusiasm, and excitement begin to flow again.

That's the reward for counting the cost. The bottom line is not giving up anything that would aid us, but everything that encumbers us, and exchanging it for the power of Christ. Then we become unencumbered, salty saints, knowing that whatever we need will be provided.

Kingdom Thinking

1. Looking back on your Christian walk, have there been any surprises for which you were unprepared when you became a Christian? What resources brought you through such situations—yours or God's?

2. We often hear the admonition, "Let go and let God." Does this mean we sit around and do nothing? Word for yourself a motto that includes complete trust, dependence on the Lord's power and faithful action.

3. After reading 2 Corinthians 12:7-10 (below), picture how you will face life's challenges, living out verse 10 in particular.

Related Readings

2 Kings 6:8-17 Psalm 121 2 Corinthians 12:7-10

Prayer to the King

Deliver me, O Father, from the chains of self-sufficiency and save me from the pride of possessions, that I may make room in my life for Your priorities and call on the power of Your Spirit to overcome the evil one. In Your strong name I pray, Amen.

18

Servant-Sized Faith

SCRIPTURE READING:

And the apostles said to the Lord, "Increase our faith!" And the Lord said, "If you had faith like a mustard seed, you would say to this mulberry tree, 'Be uprooted and be planted in the sea'; and it would obey you."

LUKE 17:5,6

This saying of Jesus' about mustard seed faith is often used to challenge us to believe great things and thus achieve great things. And in a certain sense, faith is a force mighty enough to tear down strongholds. But in context, the faith of which Jesus speaks here is not a *quantity* of belief that can work the miracle of moving a literal mountain. The saying about mustard seed faith is followed by the parable of the unworthy servant who should expect to serve his master, not his master to serve him. It is a life position that requires a special *quality* of faith to move the mountains that obscure our vision of how to relate to God. It is a lesson important enough to devote three chapters to understanding what the Lord is saying.

I was called to the hospital late at night. A highly respected member of my congregation was suffering from a terminal disease and was not expected to live. When I arrived, I found that his room was next to an infamous criminal. The criminal had been shot in an exchange of gunfire while he was being arrested for robbery, but he was expected to live.

In the waiting room, I tried to give comfort and courage to the wife of my church member, but she was virtually inconsolable. "Listen, pastor," she said. "You'd better talk to God. There are two people on this floor in serious condition. One is going to live and the other die. It's not fair! That criminal has no right to live, and my husband has. He's spent his life working for God. He deserves a break. God owes him a big, fat miracle, and I expect you to tell Him so. If that criminal lives and my husband dies, it will prove there's no justice or reward in this life!"

Mustard seed faith is faith that can grow from a tiny seed into servant-sized faith. This quality of faith had led the church member in the hospital to a life of service, without expecting any preferential treatment from his Master. Unfortunately, the man's wife lacked that kind of faith. We hear her understanding of how faith should work expressed in many ways. When tragedy strikes, this kind of faith often asks, "What did I do to deserve this? After all I've done for God and people, why did this happen to me?"

The same confused convictions pervade our relationships: "I give and give, and nobody seems to appreciate my efforts." "Nobody seems to recognize my efforts—my kids, my fellow workers, my friends at church. What's the use?"

Have you ever felt that way? Who hasn't? We expect rewards. It's built into our system of give and take. Life has its duties, relationships their obligations and work its responsibilities. But shouldn't we expect something in return? Most of us love to be loved, give to receive, work to be praised and want to be paid handsomely. From our childhood training and the conditioning of some schools of psychology, we have learned to respond to "strokes"; we are patterned by pats on the back.

Mustard seed faith stands in bold contradiction to all these feelings and desires. Of course, Jesus believed in the power of affirmation. He gave people a liberating image of who they were because of God's love. But He did not teach a system of bartered goodness and rewards. The faith of which He spoke moves us to obedience because of who He is, not because of what He can do for us. Loving us unconditionally, He does not love us any more after our good works. There is no place for the kind of faith that says, "I've got a right to a blessing because of what I've done for You."

My friend in the hospital died the next day. God did not pull off the miracle the wife felt her husband deserved. But the Lord did not owe him a special blessing—his life had been full of them. What his wife had never understood was that the good things he had done were out of gratitude, not for special preference. He believed in Christ and had served faithfully, out of love. I am persuaded that God was glad to receive him into the fulfillment and consummation of the eternal life that had begun years before his death. This assurance made him the relentless servant of God he had been.

Kingdom Thinking

1. How does love that is withheld in order to receive something damage human relationships?

2. In your opinion, do the accolades and honor bestowed on great Christian leaders unduly foster the idea that they deserve special recognition, or are such testimonials merely giving honor to whom honor is due?

3. Can you imagine any reasons why God might allow the robber in the hospital to live?

Related Readings

Psalm 103:8-10 Matthew 5:43-45 Luke 13:1-5

Prayer to the King

We are so accustomed to rewards for services rendered, dear Lord, that we need Your help in strengthening our faith. Grant that we may love You and serve You because of who You are, not because of what You can do in return for our service. Through Christ our Lord, Amen.

19

"Does Job Fear God for Nothing?"

SCRIPTURE READING:

Which of you, having a slave plowing or tending sheep, will say to him when he has come in from the field, "Come immediately and sit down to eat"? But will he not say to him, "Prepare something for me to eat,...until I have eaten and drunk"?

LUKE 17:7,8

Not long ago, one of the most generous contributors to our church cut back his contributions. He did not think he was properly thanked for his giving. The question I posed to him was why he gave: gratitude to God, or for human recognition?

In a similar way, following up on His saying about

mustard seed faith (see Luke 17:5,6), Jesus poses to us the question about why we serve Him. Does a slave serve his master in the field in order to come in and be served by the master? It is the same question Satan asked about God's faithful servant Job. God had blessed Job so richly that the tempter asked the Lord, "Does Job fear God for nothing?" (Job 1:9). Then followed the loss of all Job's wealth and family in the famous test that showed that Job's faith, though threatened, was not destroyed by his deprivation.

But what about us? Do we serve God for nothing? Some time ago I took a special course on fund-raising. We were taught how to raise support for the church by showing appreciation. The expert in funding indicated that people give when what they give is appreciated and recognized. I was not disturbed by that, because affirming people is basic to my ministry. But I couldn't help but wonder why the people of God needed to be coddled and cajoled to do what was elemental to their discipleship.

B. F. Skinner has shown us the power of reinforcement, or lack of it, for behavior modification. Eric Berne has exposed the games people play, and revealed the power of strengthening strokes. We all know about the enabling initiative of affirmation to encourage people in a pattern of behavior that is in keeping with what we want from them.

When we project all this onto God, it becomes telltale evidence that we do not serve Him for nothing. Our belief is that we can store up a spiritual savings account to draw on when life levels its blows. We think our goodness conditions His grace in our crises. But the parable of the unworthy servant stands in bold contradiction. Jesus taught that we are servants, and that servants simply do their duty.

The disciples were beginning to come to grips with the cost of following Jesus. No wonder they exclaimed, "Increase our faith!" (Luke 17:5). The saying about being able to uproot a tree and cast it into the sea indicated that limitless power was available to them. But how should it be used, and for what purpose? An intimate relationship with God alone could direct the dynamic. Absolute obedience to Him would be required. Most of all, their use of faith in the performance of deeds of mercy would not earn status with God. He could not love them more than He did already. There would be no place for an "I've got a right to desire a blessing for my use of faith" idea of entitled preference.

The *King James Version* translates Luke 17:10, "When ye shall have done all those things which are commanded you, say, We are unprofitable servants: we have done that which was our duty to do." Duty is not a popular word in our time. We would rather hear about freedom and grace these days. And it's true that what we do does not earn salvation. But the result is that many of us do very little. We gather in churches every Sunday to collect "unemployment compensation." The sanctuary is a "duty free" shop for bargains.

But an inventory of our duty to God can be helpful. We should not need special rewards for honesty, integrity, righteousness and justice. Expressing love and forgiveness should not be a big thing. Feeding the hungry and caring for the poor doesn't warrant a brass band recognition. Prayer, tithing, involvement in the church, extending the kingdom of God to every realm of society—all this should be considered the Christian's basic duty to God and others, as normal as breathing, eating and sleeping. When we've accomplished all this, we are still at the starting line, ready to begin the race of adventuresome Christianity.

Satan asked the wrong question about Job, and about us. The real question is: Do we serve God for *God?*

Kingdom Thinking

1. Do you have some normal duties—perhaps in the realm of everyday work, family living or church—that are hard for you to consider as duties because you actually delight in them?

2. Do you think duty to God and others is underemphasized these days? How can doing what we ought to do be encouraged without being legalistic or falling

into the trap of salvation by works?

3. What do you think about rewarding children for good behavior? Does it send them the message that they should do good only when rewarded? How can we communicate goodness motivated by gratitude?

Related Readings

Job 2:1,2 Romans 6:15-18 Ephesians 2:8-10

Prayer to the King

Dear Father, in my better moments I serve You because I love You, and delight in the awesome honor of welcoming You into my heart and life just to be in Your presence. Help me neither to trade on Your grace by shirking my duty, nor to elevate doing my duty to earn my salvation. Through Jesus Christ our Lord, Amen.

20

All This and Heaven, Too!

SCRIPTURE READING:

"And afterward you will eat and drink"? He does not thank the slave because he did the things which were commanded, does he? So you too, when you do all the things which are commanded you, say, "We are unworthy slaves; we have done only that which we ought to have done."

LUKE 17:8-10

When we move beyond thinking of doing our duty as something for which we should be rewarded, we find that beyond duty is delight! And delight transforms how we do our duties. Faith becomes its own reward. Putting God first and expecting nothing in return enables a breakthrough of joy, and deliverance from duty-bound living.

The psalmist had discovered this truth: "I delight to do Thy will, O my God; Thy law is within my heart" (Ps. 40:8). The apostle Paul caught the exuberance: "For I delight in the law of God, in my inmost self" (Rom. 7:22, *RSV*). He went on to say that his delight was constantly at war with the lesser motivation of obligation. We all know what that's like. We need a fresh release each day to live our lives motivated by love alone, not by calculated performance for earned reward. Delighting in God Himself, and what He's done for us, transforms how we do our duties. It does not exonerate us from responsibility; it enthuses us to live and act in response to God's amazing grace.

This is what Paul tried to communicate to the Corinthians: "For the love of Christ controls us, having concluded this, that one died for all, therefore all died; and He [Christ] died for all, that they who live should no longer live for themselves, but for Him who died and rose again on their behalf" (2 Cor. 5:14,15). The word translated "controls" here means not only that Christ's love holds us, but also that it is our compelling, driving force. It is the instigation and inspiration of the Christian life. We want to please God because He has shown His pleasure in us. The fulfillment of our duty is an expression of gratitude.

Yet another wonderful stage can be enjoyed in serving God for nothing. When we delight in serving the Master, we can go on to become His friends. At the close of His ministry, Christ ushered His disciples into a level of friendship that would liberate their lives as servants of God. "No longer do I call you servants, for a servant does not know what his master is doing; but I have called you friends, for all things that I heard from My Father I have made known to you" (John 15:15, *NKJV*).

Just as delight gives us enthusiasm for doing our duty, so friendship with the Master gives us power to serve. It is not just for enjoyment, but also for our employment—in discipleship. When we realize that we are undeserving servants whom Christ has saved from a meaningless, wasted, frustrated life to a life of purpose, joy and hope, we will want to be instruments through whom He will do the same for other people.

But as if delight and friendship with Jesus aren't enough, there is heaven, too! Luke 17:8 closes with a reference to the wonderful fact that "afterward you will eat and drink." When Christ returns, those who have served with joy, out of love and not for reward, will after all be rewarded at His banquet. "Blessed are those slaves whom the master shall find on the alert when he comes; truly I say to you, that he will gird himself to serve, and have them recline at the table, and will come up and wait on them" (Luke 12:37).

That is the glorious picture of the Second Coming,

and also of the blessing of heaven. The One who was a servant on our behalf on the Cross, who washed the disciples' feet to show them how to serve Him by humbly caring for each other, will welcome us, His mere servants, as honored guests!

Until then, the sheer joy and delight of being His obedient servants enables us to pray with an old Scot friend of mine: "Lord, this is John, reporting in for duty."

Kingdom Thinking

1. Can you recall a time in your Christian experience—perhaps when you first accepted Christ personally—when duty and joy seemed to be perfectly blended. Is the joy still present? If not, what would it take to re-create it?

2. How do you typically begin each day? Does your morning routine lend itself to taking on the day in a fresh frame of mind? If not, how can you change it?

3. Do you think of Jesus not only as Lord, but also as your *friend*? Picture yourself and a friend doing what you enjoy doing together. Now substitute Jesus for the friend. Does the picture still seem natural for you? If not, how can it become more natural?

Related Readings

Psalm 100 Philippians 2:5-11 Revelation 21:1-4

Prayer to the King

What a joy to be Your servant, Holy Father! Help me to remember that a day in Your kingdom as Your servant is better than a lifetime as a mere king outside Your house. Shield me from arrogance and false pride, and from the delusion that true joy is to be found anywhere other than in Your service. In Jesus' name, Amen.

21

Shrewd Saints

SCRIPTURE READING:

The steward said to himself, "What shall I do, since my master is taking the stewardship away from me?...I know what I shall do, so that when I am removed from the stewardship, they will receive me into their homes."...And his master praised the unrighteous steward because he had acted shrewdly; for the sons of this age are more shrewd in relation to their own kind than the sons of light.

LUKE 16:3,4,8

We are startled that Jesus would commend a servant who had been so deceitful. He had been caught using his master's money for his own pleasure, and while his master's debtors thought he was still employed, he endeared himself to them by drastically discounting what they owed (see Luke 16:5-7). He had to make friends at any cost in order to have a few favors to collect when he was discharged. Perhaps a grateful debtor would take him into his own business.

To grasp this parable by the jugular vein, we must remember that parables were taught by Jesus to focus on one point. This parable is not an allegory in which each aspect and character is representative of facets of the homily. When we look for the one thing Jesus was trying to communicate to His disciples, and to us, we will see that He did not commend unrighteousness, but *shrewdness*. While we are not told whether the employer reinstated the servant to his position, it is clear that he praised him for his astuteness.

Seated on a cross-country flight with one of America's most successful businessmen, I was shocked by his frank reply when I asked him the secret of his success. "Shrewdness!" was his one-word reply. He went on to say that he spent every waking hour thinking, scheming, planning, developing and putting deals together. In it all, he tried to be completely honest, but all the power of his intellect, the strength of his seemingly limitless energies, the determination of his iron will, and the resources of his calculated discernment of people were employed to accomplish his goals.

When it seemed natural and unforced, I shifted our conversation into what the man believed about God. There was a long silence. He admitted that he had not taken any time to think about that aspect of life. He was astonished by my response: "If you ever put the same time, energy and will into being a disciple of Jesus Christ, you would be a contemporary Apostle Paul."

The man's response was thoughtful and reflective: "Nobody has ever challenged me with that!"

Jesus challenges us with something similar in this parable. He commends shrewdness and single-hearted purpose, not dishonesty in billing! Shrewdness has taken on a negative blight in our time. But the word actually means keen, artful, astute, innovative. In substance, the Lord was saying, "Listen: why is it that the children of darkness scheme and plan and manipulate, and you hardly give a flippant thought to God and His strategy for the world?"

The steward, unrighteous though he was, saw things as they were, and dealt with them decisively. He was about to lose his job, the books had to be turned in, and he had to find a way to save his neck. Jesus wants us to come to grips with life's hard realities in a similar way. He wants us to recognize the crucial issues of life. Where will we spend eternity? What will our books show about how we handled the Lord's resources? How are we spending the years of our lives in order to live forever with Him? Can we see not only the problems, but also the potential?

Shrewdness produces an energetic, sagacious plan

to solve life's problems. Shrewdness does not say, "There's no hope. It's all over now. What's the use of trying?" Jesus affirms the part of us that is willing to dare to believe that nothing is too big for God. He wants people to see difficulties as a dynamic prelude to new advancement of His kingdom. He wants us to use our intellect, emotion and will to devise a plan that will astound us and those around us.

A financier in our congregation has an uncanny sense of trends in thought and what will sell. We are blessed because he uses this shrewdness to strategize new ways of setting creative goals and plans for our urban church. He sees potential.

From this parable, I think we learn a secret about this dynamic servant of the Lord. The source of his shrewdness is none other than the Holy Spirit!

Kingdom Thinking

1. Why does "shrewdness" have negative connotations for many of us?

2. Give examples of how these characteristics of shrewdness can be applied to meeting challenges or crises faced by the Church, or individually in your life:

- Keen—
- Artful—
- Astute—
- Innovative—

Related Readings

1 Kings 3:5-12 Proverbs 1:20-23 James 1:5-7

Prayer to the King

Bless us, dear Lord, with wisdom and holy shrewdness as we face the crises of life, and with optimism as we face the problems of life. Keep us from assuming that astuteness is a worldly trait, and help us to become more focused and intense about serving You. In Jesus' name, Amen.

22

Wringing Righteousness from Riches

SCRIPTURE READING:

And I say to you, make friends for yourselves by means of the mammon of unrighteousness; that when it fails, they may receive you into the eternal dwellings. If therefore you have not been faithful in the use of unrighteous mammon, who will entrust the true riches to you?

LUKE 16:9,11

Unjust though he was, the steward to whom we were introduced in the preceding chapter had a plan. He knew that if he did nothing, he would soon be destitute and friendless. So he moved decisively to trade his careless handling of his master's funds for friendship with those who might be able to help him when his fraud had been discovered.

Jesus is asking, "If a self-serving steward could use money to gain friends, why can't the children of light use it to make true friends? If the unjust steward can use mammon, or material goods, for unrighteous purposes, why cannot the righteous use it to make friends for God?" Jesus wants us to use our material resources as an expression of our own friendship with God, in order to make others His friends.

This is the purpose of tithing and giving to Christian causes. Our money is used to support activities and programs that introduce people to the Savior, and to care for their needs in His name and for His glory. That is the standard we should apply when we decide how to distribute our money. We must be assured that as a result of our giving, people will become friends of the Lord through an experience of His love and forgiveness. Giving for ministries to alleviate human suffering must also include a concern for people's eternal salvation.

Often this giving attitude can become very personal. We must look for opportunities not simply to give to the church program, but also to seek specific opportunities to become involved with people to whom we want to introduce God as their friend, caring for them personally and being a friend to them ourselves. God entrusts us with both material and spiritual resources to use not just for church budgets, but also for befriending *people*. When we do this, we experience the Lord's promise: It is more blessed to give than to receive.

Jesus was not opposed to money. But He did know that it had the power to displace God in our lives. It's the first of the false gods. That's why He insisted that we use money to make friends for God. Heaven should be full of people who will cheer us when we enter. There should be hundreds who will call out joyously, saying, "Welcome home. We are here because of you! You gave of yourself and your resources so that we could know the Savior and live eternally. Thanks for being you!"

The thrust of verse 11 is the sobering message that our preparation for greater riches—greater spiritual blessings as well as the riches of heaven—is to use what earthly riches we have faithfully, for God's glory. This includes our gifts, talents, influence and opportunities, as well as our money.

Project yourself into God's position of oversight of the world and the distribution of His immense resources of spiritual and material power. From His point of view, would we consider ourselves worthy of further investment? Are we good risks, as evidenced by using what He blesses us with to make friends for Him?

A man confided an experience he had while going through his checks at income tax time. He was facing an excruciating divorce. He and his wife drifted away from the Lord and each other. His analysis of his checks over the past year unsettled him. He said, "I've just gone through what we spent last year. If I would have done that six months ago, I could have predicted the dilemma I'm in right now. So much money was spent on our own pleasure and luxury, and a pittance on the needs of others. Our self-indulgence has distorted our values. No wonder we lost our purpose and direction."

Perhaps we should "go through our checks," too. Has our spending brought us closer to or farther from God? Has our use of our material resources accounted for the salvation and alleviation of suffering for any person this past year?

Kingdom Thinking

1. We hear a great deal these days about the need to enable those who are helped with their material needs to "preserve their dignity." What is meant by this? What are some examples of how this can be done?

2. Do you make a practice of tithing—giving 10 percent of your income to "make friends for God"? If not, how do you decide what part of your earnings to dedicate to God and His work?

3. What are some needs in your community that your church could help meet? If the group can reach a consensus, consider approaching your church's pastor or a ministry team with a plan for reaching out in this way.

Related Readings

1 Corinthians 8:1-7 1 Corinthians 9:6-12

Prayer to the King

Dear Lord, we confess our tendency to value material goods and wealth over spiritual riches, and to lavish luxury on ourselves while overlooking human need. Grant us a sense of Your way of valuing things and people, so that we may be stirred to introduce those who do not know You to the riches of Your friendship. Through Christ our Lord, Amen.

23

A Man Who Loved Little

SCRIPTURE READING:

And Jesus answered and said to him, "Simon, I have something to say to you." And he replied, "Say it, Teacher." "A certain moneylender had two debtors: one owed five hundred denarii, and the other fifty. When they were unable to repay, he graciously forgave them both. Which of them therefore will love him more?...He who is forgiven little, loves little."

LUKE 7:40-42,47

We are in the banquet hall in Simon the Pharisee's house. Invited guests are arriving, mostly scribes and Pharisees and community nobles. Simon greets each one with a welcoming kiss. Servants wash their feet. After they are reclined at the table, each is anointed with oil.

Jesus of Nazareth has been invited, too. He leans forward to receive Simon's customary kiss of welcome, only to find the host rigidly aloof. A servant who has brought a towel and basin for Jesus' feet is motioned off. The guests smile and look at each other with knowing glances. It dawns on us that Jesus is not a guest so much as the subject of an inquest. It is time for these Pharisees to investigate the claims people are making about His healing the sick, opening the eyes of the blind and exorcising evil spirits.

Simon does not wait long to begin the inquiry. He and other Pharisees want to know about the people's claim that He is a prophet. Others raise questions about His breaking the Sabbath, and His claim to have the authority to forgive sins.

At the height of the dispute, we are shocked to see that an uninvited guest has slipped into the hall. Moving boldly to the banquet table, she suddenly produces an alabaster flask from her robes. Our attention is riveted as we watch her kneel at Jesus' feet. What is she doing? Would she dare? Yes! The woman anoints Jesus' feet both with her tears and with oil from the flask. Then she scandalously releases the tresses of her hair to wipe her tears from Jesus' feet, kissing them as though He were a king. Simon is enraged. "If this man were a prophet," he said to himself, "He would know who and what sort of person this woman is who is touching Him, that she is a sinner" (Luke 7:39).

It is then that Jesus confronts Simon with the parable of the two debtors. Simon seems to know that Jesus is cornering him in front of his friends, but there is nothing to do but point out the obvious: the debtor who was forgiven more would love more—and when Jesus points out Simon's painfully embarrassing breach of hospitality in verses 44-48, the Pharisee knows all too well that Jesus has identified him as the one who loved little.

What had happened to Simon to cause him to earn this unenviable identification? He had much to be thankful for. All that he had and was able to accomplish was a gift of God. Could it be that he had witnessed the sacrifices of the Temple without the experience that they were meant for him personally? Even though he may have disagreed with Jesus, how could he be so inhospitable to such a teacher as He was?

Like it or not, many of us must admit we can identify with Simon's level of love. We have a level of gratitude that never gets beyond self-satisfaction. We are grateful to God for all He has done, but *we never break out of the cycle of the idea that God has blessed us because we are good.*

Simon was a good person. His position demanded that he be superior in knowledge and religious practices. His problem was that he could not love. He forgot that he had been blessed to be a blessing. His position required that he maintain an image, so he could not admit that he was imperfect. And if all of life's energy is spent on keeping up a front, then God and His blessings become part of the props of refortification rather than something for which to be thankful. Simon felt no need to be forgiven much; therefore, he could not love much.

The implication for us is that if our carefully constructed righteousness has led to self-sufficiency, we will begin to believe that God is privileged to have us among His chosen people. We lose sight of our need of atonement for our subtle sins. The mystery of our nature is that the more we grow in moral strength and character development, the further we may go from the Source. Pride always runs up a monstrous debt with God. The sign that we are overextended in this debt is that we think someone else needs forgiveness more than we do. And the tragedy is that if we cannot confess how great a debtor we are, we cannot allow the Lord to speak to us that final word spoken to the woman at the banquet: "Your faith has saved you; go in peace" (v. 50).

Kingdom Thinking

1. Don't the "Simons" of the world get some credit

for disciplining themselves in righteous living? What was the problem with Simon's righteousness?

2. As you read this parable, with whom did you identify the most? Why?

3. Do you think modern religious people are too aloof from and out of touch with people such as the woman who barged into Simon's house? What is required to minister to such people?

Related Readings

Psalm 41:1-4 Proverbs 16:18 Romans 4:3-8

Prayer to the King

Help us to share in Your righteousness, dear Father, without becoming self-righteous. Help us not to be so focused on maintaining a favorable image before others that we forget what great debtors we are, and how we depend totally on Your grace. And having been forgiven much, help us to love Him much, in whose name we pray, Amen.

24

A Woman Who Loved Much

SCRIPTURE READING:

"Her sins, which are many, have been forgiven, for she loved much;..." And He said to her, "Your sins have been forgiven." And those who were reclining at the table with Him began to say to themselves, "Who is this man who even forgives sins?" And He said to the woman, "Your faith has saved you; go in peace."

LUKE 7:47,48-50

In Simon the Pharisee's banquet hall, a permissive Palestinian custom made it possible for the woman to slip in, uninvited. The murmuring gossip informs us that she is a woman of the streets whom this Jesus had spoken with the day before, claiming to have forgiven her. She huddles unobtrusively against the wall, fearing discovery and exposure. The woman's demeanor shows the brokenness of the years, but there is a radiance that shines on her face—unmistakable evidence that she has taken His word of forgiveness seriously. Even more than that, we observe a fulfilled look about her, as if the years of longing for true love had finally been satisfied.

Jesus could have met the woman's embarrassing display of affection and honor with a polite smile of dismissal, turning to the others at the table to direct attention elsewhere. Instead, He looks at her with gratitude and compassion. He accepts her gift of love. There is affirmation and assurance in His face as His eyes meet hers. The whole banquet is disrupted; Simon is enraged.

After engaging His host in the parable of the two debtors, Jesus addresses Simon with relentless discernment. "I entered your house; you gave Me no water for My feet, but she has wet My feet with her tears, and wiped them with her hair. You gave Me no kiss; but she, since the time I came in, has not ceased to kiss My feet. You did not anoint My head with oil, but she anointed My feet with perfume" (Luke 7:44-46). Jesus' first pronouncement is to Simon: "Her sins, which are many, have been forgiven, for she loved much" (v. 47). Then He turns to the woman herself and the tender love and unlimited grace of heaven saturate His words: "Your sins have been forgiven" (v. 48), a reaffirmation of the previous absolution.

We observe the new dignity in the woman's carriage as she leaves the banquet hall. Having owed the Master much, she has expressed much love. Her experience of His forgiveness the day before had brought her there to express her irrepressible thanksgiving; now her assurance of His acceptance in the presence of the official leaders of the village sends her away, bursting with praise and joy.

The woman has taught us that gratitude is both the true motivation for love and the result of forgiveness. She loved profoundly because she had been forgiven immensely. The forgiven woman becomes our mentor. The warm and gracious people of the world are those who are conscious of how much they have been forgiven. The greater the depths of contrition, the higher the heights of compassion. When we know that we are sinners saved by grace, we become lovers who communicate hope to others.

The woman could not do enough to express her gratitude. She had to find a sacrament to express her love. Nothing was too demanding. The danger of ridicule, the fear of judgment from Simon and his ilk, the shame of public exposure of her sordid past were of little concern in comparison to her dominant need to thank the Master. When she witnessed the preposterous lack of respect and consideration shown Him by

Simon, she had to balance the scales. The whole world needed to share her adoration.

Some of us can identify with the woman immediately. We may not be implicated in her particular sin, but we know that our own brand is no less culpable. The result is the same: God will not bless the mess we have made of the gift of life. But the story flashes with the lightning of unmerited favor, the thunder of forgiving love. There is no depth to which we can fall that our Lord will not stoop to find us and reclaim us. There is nothing we can do or say that will negate Christ's love—except the pride of Simon.

Only a sinner needs a Savior. Jesus gave His beatific benediction to the woman, not to Simon. His blessing "Go in peace" (v. 50) means, "Go into an ever-increasing experience of God's unifying, healing wholeness." We arise from having expressed our gratitude to extend His message of forgiveness to others. Costly involvement, listening with love, forgiveness as we have been forgiven, second chances when they are least deserved, sacrificial giving of our resources for practical help, sharing the hope we have discovered in the gospel—all are ways to show our gratitude for the word of His grace.

Kingdom Thinking

1. The Greek word for "confess" is *homologeo*,

meaning to "say after." True confession is to allow the Lord to tell us what we need to confess. If we followed His guidance in our confessions today, what would we confess?

2. How are receiving forgiveness and forgiving others related? Can we have one without the other? (Read Matt. 6:14,15.)

3. What Bible figure saw himself as "the chief of sinners" (see 1 Tim. 1:15)? Explain how he showed that he also "loved much."

Related Readings

Isaiah 57:14-16 Romans 2:21-23 1 John 1:8-10

Prayer to the King

Create in me, O Lord, a heart that is quicker to see sin in my own life than in the lives of others. Help me not to block Your forgiveness by pride and self-righteousness. Praise to You for being a God who dwells in the hearts of those who can confess their need for You and Your grace. May that grace make me both a forgiven and a forgiving person. In Jesus' name, Amen.

25

Loving Beyond the Rules

SCRIPTURE READING:

A certain man was going down from Jerusalem to Jericho; and he fell among robbers, and they stripped him and beat him, and went off leaving him half dead. And by chance a certain priest was going down on that road, and when he saw him, he passed by on the other side. And likewise a Levite also, when he came to the place and saw him, passed by on the other side.

LUKE 10:30-32

Jesus told this famous parable of the good Samaritan in response to a religious lawyer's question, "Teacher, what shall I do to inherit eternal life?" (Luke 10:25).

No doubt, Jesus has observed His religious questioner carefully. His official robes declare his position, and his bearing communicates the assurance of refined legalism. At the center of his forehead is a meticulously positioned phylactery—a small, black, calfskin box bound tightly with leather thongs. Sacred, Old Testament passages were carried there, in response to Deuteronomy 6:8: "They shall be as frontals on your forehead."

Jesus' answer shows that He knows the man to be knowledgeable in the Law. "How does it read to you?" He asks (v. 26). And He is ready for the legalist's further question, "Who is my neighbor?" (v. 29). Quite appropriately, the Lord chooses two very legally correct types—a priest and a Levite—to help answer the question the lawyer *should* have asked: "How should I act as a neighbor?"

As a matter of fact, the priest and Levite were behaving as the law specified. They were busy about God's work, hurrying to Jericho down the "Bloody Way," as the twenty-two-mile road had come to be known. It was a precarious road because of robbers who hid among the rocks and caves.

But it was not just the danger that caused the pair of religiously correct men to pass by the wounded man. He had been left "half dead" (v. 30), and for them to touch a dead body would have rendered them ceremonially unclean for twenty-four hours. We must understand that the needs of a person in pain were secondary to being on time and ceremonially prepared to officiate at a religious ritual. Those were the rules, at least in the eyes of these proper religious functionaries.

And, of course, this is precisely the point of the parable. When "the rules" seem to dictate that we overlook needy people, we need to look again at our interpretation of the rules. A story is told of a man in India, rushing home to his family to tell of his conversion to Christianity. He stumbled over a poor beggar in the streets who pleaded for help. He later confessed that he told the man he was sorry he could not stop to help, because he had to get home to share the joy of his new relationship with Christ.

We are aghast and critical in response to such an incident, and to the behavior of the priest and the Levite in Jesus' parable. Then it occurs to us that there have been times for all of us when our enthusiasm for what we perceived to be the rules of religion has precluded specific concern for people in need. In this parable, the Lord is testing the authenticity of our love for Him by our willingness to engage in practical caring for others.

And, of course, Jesus doesn't help the composure of the religious lawyer by choosing a Samaritan as the hero of the story. The Jews abhorred this half-breed people in the northern part of Palestine. They were descendants of a remnant of Jews left in the land when most were dragged off into Babylonian exile in 722 B.C. Those who remained, intermarried with Assyrians brought in to occupy the land. They even had their own temple. The hostility of the Jews for the Samaritans generated through the years was at a high pitch in Jesus' day.

All this enables Jesus to drive home the point of the parable: God's love is never limited by the rules of religion. The world Jesus came to save was a Jericho road, and His response to human suffering was in marked contrast to the calculated neglect and qualified concern of religious people. It is the despised half-breed who fulfills the summary of the law that the lawyer had so glibly repeated (see v. 27). It was the Samaritan who loved his neighbor as himself, he who fulfilled the deeper meaning of the great commandment.

Because we, too, are religious people who want to live by the rules, we cannot read this parable without asking: Would we—*do* we—use our religion to pass by on the other side, leaving the wounded, the debilitated and the hurting to suffer by our benign neglect?

Kingdom Thinking

1. If you were telling such a parable today, who would you use to fill the roles of the priest and the Levite?

2. What opportunities do you have before you to

respond as did the Samaritan? Make a list. What could you do, say or give to live out the message of this parable?

3. Read Galatians 5:22,23 regarding the fruit of the Spirit. Which of these character traits of Christ, enabled in us by the Holy Spirit, do you need most for each of the challenges you focused on in the previous question?

Related Readings

Leviticus 19:13-18 Romans 13:8-10 James 2:14-20

Prayer to the King

Holy Father, help us to love to do Your will and to practice our faithfulness to You; but grant that we may not use our desire to be right to obscure what is right to do toward our neighbor. Help us to respect the rules, but to keep them in their place by following the ultimate rule of love. In the name of Him who first loved us, Amen.

26

Who Is My Neighbor?

SCRIPTURE READING:

And behold, a certain lawyer stood up and put Him to the test, saying, "Teacher, what shall I do to inherit eternal life?" And He said to him, "What is written in the Law? How does it read to you?" And he answered and said, "You shall love the Lord your God with all your heart, and with all your soul, and with all your strength, and with all your mind; and your neighbor as yourself."...But wishing to justify himself, he said to Jesus, "And who is my neighbor?"

LUKE 10:25-29

Even though the religious lawyer is trifling with Jesus and putting Him "to the test," the question is very real.

As we listen to Jesus' parable of the good Samaritan, we are astonished by the way he recasts the question, transposing it from a philosophical to a practical issue. Apart from the parable's pointed criticism of elevating rules over people, as we noted in the previous chapter, Jesus wants us to see that we ourselves are on the Jericho road, and that anyone in need is our neighbor.

The needy are all about us. They are those who have been debilitated physically, psychologically or socially by no fault of their own. Who is the "certain man" on the road for me? Is he or she a member of my own family, among my friends, at work, in our church, in our community? We are challenged to put ourselves in the parable. We can be wounders or passersby or wound healers. Jesus will have accomplished His purpose in the parable if we identify the wounded in our lives and act toward them in ways that express the spontaneous love portrayed in the Samaritan's immediate and uncalculating response.

Our first response may be that we simply cannot respond to all the needs we see. Often, after I have spent a long Sunday preaching in two services in the morning, some needy person is waiting at the door or by my car in the parking lot. Everything within me longs to escape and go home for a leisurely time with my family. The only way I have been able to handle the limitless demands of people is to surrender my time and energy to the Lord, acknowledge that He knows how much I can take and offer help in unreserved response. It takes more energy to calculate whom I will help than it does just to trust the Lord to provide the wisdom and strength I need to help anyone whom He places in my path.

We should be amazed by the way the Lord answers the question, Who is my neighbor? by the miraculous way He weaves together the destiny of different individuals. He will send us the people we need when we are wounded, and He will place us in the lives of those who are wounded when He wants to love through us. Suddenly, with that definition of "neighbor," life takes on a new quality. People with needs are not a burden; they are gifts of God for us to give away what He has given us. The purpose of our lives is to be an expression of His spontaneous love.

We simply cannot define "neighbor" in this way if our relationship with God is based on the fulfillment of the rules and regulations of our religion more than on the genuine needs of hurting people. As we have seen, this was the error of the priest and the Levite. True religion does not exclude certain people from qualifying as our neighbor on conditions of propriety. When that happens, religious folk are really more wounded than the man they passed by. They are beaten spiritually by the system, more than the man had been beaten physically by the robbers. Traditions and formalism take a terrible toll on the capacity to care personally for others.

To the lawyer's credit, he can answer Jesus correctly when he asks, "Which of these three do you think proved to be a neighbor?" (Luke 10:36). There was only one obvious answer: "The one who showed mercy." Now Jesus shifts the emphasis from a story about someone else to a personal question with undeniable force: "Go and do the same" (v. 37). Suddenly, we feel what the lawyer must have felt. Once we say we believe in Jesus as Lord and Savior, we are immediately called into a demanding, challenging, but very exciting "go and do likewise" adventure of unstudied, spontaneous love. The wounded of the world—our neighbors—are our agenda.

The Lord repeatedly comes to us on the Jericho road in the form of the lost, lonely, frustrated, fearful, beaten and battered people of the world. Our response to these our neighbors is our response to Him.

Kingdom Thinking

1. People in emergency health care speak of "triage"—the often painful process of deciding whom to help on the basis of the most urgent need or the best chances of survival. Do the numbers of needy "neighbors" about us seem to demand that we make similar decisions? How do we decide who is on the Lord's agenda for us to care for and help?

2. How have modern times and technology broad-

ened the definition of "neighbor"? How does this fit with Jesus' words, "As you did it to one of the least of these my brethren, you did it to me" (Matt. 25:40, *RSV*)?

3. Is helping people always easy? Have you experienced any difficulty in trying to offer help to a needy person?

4. What is the Christian's responsibility when people "take advantage" of proffered help?

Related Readings

Deuteronomy 15:7-11 Luke 14:12-14
James 1:27—2:4

Prayer to the King

Dear Lord, we are often so overwhelmed with tending to our own needs that we forget the more critical needs all about us. From the highest halls of government to the simple, single acts of individuals, help us to be neighbors to each other in a way that builds up Your kingdom. Through Christ the King we pray, Amen.

27

How to Know God's Will

SCRIPTURE READING:

A man had two sons, and he came to the first and said, "Son, go work today in the vineyard." And he answered and said, "I will, sir"; and he did not go. And he came to the second and said the same thing. But he answered and said, "I will not"; yet he afterward regretted it and went. Which of the two did the will of his father? They said, "The latter."

MATTHEW 21:28-31

No question is asked of me more often than this: "How can I know the will of God?" Discovering and doing the will of God is the only way to have a consistent experience of the abundant life Jesus came to reveal and enable in us. Yet, why is it so few people get a clear answer when they pray, "Lord, show me your will!"?

Jesus' parable of the two sons indicates that having to agonize to discover God's will is a symptom of something much deeper. Two basic assumptions guide my conversations with people who ask how they can know the will of God. The first is: If we are seeking to know the will of God, it's a sure sign that we are out of it. The second is: We cannot know the will of God unless we are willing to do the obvious, primary thing God has told us to do.

I agree with little that the German philosopher Nietzsche said, except this: "If you know your why, you'll understand your how." That's the point of this parable. Jesus has been confronted by His enemies, who asked Him who gave Him the authority to do what He did (see Matt. 21:23). In response, He asked them whether John the Baptist's baptism was of the authority of God, or of men (see v. 25). "We do not know," they said (v. 27).

But many of them did know; they knew all too well. Jesus was leading them to the point He wanted to make: How could they deal with His authority as Messiah if they had not been willing to accept the authority of the One who prepared the way for His messianic ministry?

Now we are ready for the parable. We see that Jesus'

opponents are like the son who paid lip-service to his father, but refused to go work in the vineyard. It is important to notice that these are the same people who claimed they did not know the answer to Jesus' question about John.

Their question, like ours when we say we do not know God's will, was an exposure not of their ignorance, but of their disobedience! We already know more than what we have done. We have not acted on the knowledge we have. Action is the nerve center of the spiritual life. Obedience is the opening of the thermostatic valve for spiritual power. Luther said, "I believe in order to obey; I obey in order to believe."

The discovery of the will of God comes from habitual, consistent, repetitive communion with God. If we say, "I don't know what the will of God is for my life," it means that day by day we have not been listening to the elementary guidance that results from faithful prayer and communion.

The oftrepeated words of the Lord's Prayer mock us. We say, "Your will be done, on earth as it is in heaven," when often we really are not ready to do God's will on earth. An exception to this kind of praying was a man in a congregation I once served who was determined never to say or sing more than he was willing to do. Often, I would observe him in the worshiping congregation not singing certain hymns. When I asked him about his dumbness, he said, "I'm not able to sing that yet because I'm not ready to do what the words promise." And yet, he was a man I could depend on. He would always do what he said he would do. When he pledged money, it was faithfully given. If I asked him to follow up on a potential Christian, he would never let me down. He was trustworthy.

The Lord seeks open, receptive disciples who live up to what they say they will do, in order that He may give them immediate guidance for each new challenge where the reality of the problem intersects with the resources of His Spirit. The only way to know the will of God for life's big decisions is to be willing to start today to be obedient in the little things.

If you were to ask me what my wife thinks or wants in a certain situation, I should not have to ask her. Forty-three years of marriage should give me some knowledge of her convictions, wants and desires. If I had to say, "Just a moment, I'll ask her what she has to say about that," it would say something about our marriage. I have lived, talked and prayed with my Mary Jane through the years. I know her. Should we be less sure of God and His will?

Kingdom Thinking

1. Share some specific instance in which you wish you knew more of God's will for your life. Then reflect carefully and honestly on any hesitance you may feel

about doing something you already feel some conviction about in that area.

2. Why were Jesus' opponents really reluctant to say whether John's work was from heaven or from men (see Matt. 21:24-26)?

3. How could Jesus say that sinners such as "tax-gatherers and harlots will get into the kingdom of God before you" (see vv. 31,32)?

Related Readings

Matthew 21:42-46   Luke 6:46-49   James 1:22-25

Prayer to the King

Give us the will, O God, to do what we already know of Your will, so that we may know more of it, and make it ours. Help us not to say we will do more than we are willing to do, but to make it our glad purpose to arise every day, open to entering doors You will open wider when we step through them in faith. Through Jesus Christ our Lord, Amen.

28

Life in a Vineyard

SCRIPTURE READING:

Jesus said to them, "Truly I say to you that the tax-gatherers and harlots will get into the kingdom of God before you For John came to you in the way of righteousness and you did not believe him; but the tax-gatherers and harlots did believe him; and you, seeing this, did not even feel remorse afterward so as to believe him."

MATTHEW 21:31,32

Life in the Lord's vineyard, which is His kingdom, is a life of faith and obedience. Yahweh's persistent command is, "Go into the vineyard and work. Depend on My sovereign power and do My will in all your affairs. Trust Me and I will bless you."

The responses of the two sons in this parable capture the attitudes we often express to the call of discipleship. But both categories are less than adequate. No accolade should be given to a person who says, "I will" and doesn't, or to a person who says, "I won't" but finally does. Jesus wants to lead us beyond the dualism to a third possibility. He invites us to know God so intimately and personally that as a result of that friendship we know what He wants us to do before the crises of life hit. The most natural result of companionship with God is to work in His vineyard. Why, then, should we have to be asked? If the two sons knew and loved the father, they would have known that by now the vineyard was theirs by inheritance. Why did the father have to recruit them as though they were day laborers? What a demeaning insult to him!

Life in the vineyard means habitual, consistent, repetitive communion with God without having to be asked to follow through on what we know is our responsibility. The Master of the vineyard does not unfold His complete strategy for any of us. Daily obedience alone can prepare for drastic eventualities or spectacular opportunities. The rudimentary precedes the remarkable. It is a life of faith; the next step is revealed if we take the first step. Doing the basics daily prepares us to receive strength in the momentous pressures life deals us.

The psalmist's confident expectation was, "I shall run the way of Thy commandments, for Thou wilt enlarge my heart" (Ps. 119:32). All through this psalm, the author asks for strength to do the basics so the Lord can prepare for him His blessings. Our enlarged heart is open to new vision as we make it an obedient heart.

Life in the vineyard means three things. First, it means that we care about people and their needs. We are surrounded by people who need to know about God's love, to have us express His grace in our attitudes, actions and words. The Lord has chosen us to be communicators of His gift of salvation and eternal life. People pass through the narrow gate one by one, helped by some person who has been obedient to the Master of the vineyard to share its fruits of forgiveness and the promise of a new beginning.

Second, life in the vineyard means following the obvious implications of the gospel in our relationships, responsibilities and the needs of our communities. Our families, homes, churches, places of work are the realms in which we learn how to cooperate with the Lord to get His work done.

Third, unless we have praised God for what He has shown us in our personal needs in the past, He will not give us fresh guidance. Someone has said that the present is the past rolled up for action; the past is the present unrolled for understanding. As we work in the vineyard, we must constantly affirm that it is the Lord's, not ours. He has made us recipients of the privilege of working by His strength and wisdom. Consistent thanksgiving in doing our work opens us up for greater responsibility. Again, David articulates our prayer: "I delight to do Thy will, O my God" (Ps. 40:8).

On the night before Jesus was crucified, He revealed to us what He had taught in the parable. Long before that night of anguish, life in the vineyard, in constant communion with the Father, had made the mandate of calvary clear. In the garden of Gethsemane, He did not pray to know the will of God, but for the power to do it.

Kingdom Thinking

1. What has the parable of the two sons said to you about how you respond to the Lord on a daily basis? Which son are you most like? Picture how you would live if the sheer joy of working with and for the Lord were the motive of your daily obedience.

2. What fundamental New Testament essential for salvation would be eliminated if we knew in advance every detailed step we should take (see 2 Cor. 5:7)?

3. Instead of knowing particulars of God's will, what did Paul say he sought to know in Philippians 3:8-10, and what impact do you think this had on his daily decisions?

Related Readings

Psalm 46:10,11 Matthew 14:25-31 Hebrews 11:8-10

Prayer to the King

O Lord, may my knowledge of Your forgiveness of my sins and the reassurance of Your presence be enough for me to step out in faith. Save me from fretfulness and anxiety about the details of Your will, and deliver me instead into unrestrained obedience, trust and joy. In Jesus' name, Amen.

29

The Great Equalizer

SCRIPTURE READING:

Now there was a certain rich man, and he habitually dressed in purple and fine linen, gaily living in splendor every day. And a certain poor man named Lazarus was laid at his gate, covered with sores, and longing to be fed with the crumbs which were falling from the rich man's table....Now it came about that the poor man died and he was carried away by the angels to Abraham's bosom; and the rich man also died and was buried.

LUKE 16:19-22

The parable of the rich man and Lazarus is a study in contrasts—while drawing at the same time a graphic picture of death as the great equalizer. In vivid terms, Jesus both contrasts the rich man in his purple and fine linen with Lazarus's poverty, and describes their fellowship in death. This contrast and similarity will occupy us in this chapter, and the view of eternity the story offers will be examined in the next.

Tradition has named Lazarus's partner in death *Dives*, the Latin name for "rich man." You can easily picture him. He is never seen in any haberdasheries other than the most auspicious and ostentatious. His linen undergarment coat with long sleeves was probably made of Egyptian flax, often as valuable as gold. The cloak worn over his coat was made of costly purple material. Purple was a sign of royalty or immense wealth. The dye was obtained from a purple species of mussel, at prohibitive cost to any but the most affluent and powerful.

The way Dives lived was consistent with his clothing. "Gaily living in splendor" (Luke 16:19) are Jesus' words. The Greek name means faring sumptuously or making merry magnificently. The picture is one of limitless wealth and indulgent, luxuriant prosperity—every day. Dives' feasting and frolic knew no reverence for the Sabbath or special days of fasting and prayer. No day was holy for him in his secular search for pleasure and satisfaction through all he could taste and touch.

Lazarus is a startling contrast. He was "covered with

sores" of leprosy (v. 20). The pitiful creature seems to contradict his name, which means "God is my help." This parable is the only one in which a character is given a name. The reason will become evident as the drama unfolds.

Each day, Lazarus is plopped down at Dives' gate to beg for crumbs from the wealthy man's table. The verb for "was laid" implies that he was flung there with contempt and roughness. On the other hand, the word *pylon*, for gate, intensifies the contrast between Dives' splendor and Lazarus's squalor. It means an entrance of magnificent artistry and exquisite beauty. From this, we get a hint of what Dives' mansion must have been like—a startling backdrop for Lazarus's pitiful plight.

We can imagine that Dives looked the other way each time he rode through his gates in his magnificently appointed carriage. But soon he did not see Lazarus at all. The narcotic of affluence dulled his sensitivity and awareness. Dives was no longer in touch with the reality that was focused in the anguish about him.

The disposition of their bodies at the time of death dramatizes the dreadful disparity of life. Lazarus's body would have been flung naked on the burning rubbish heap outside the city wall. Dives was no doubt buried in a tomb above ground, reserved for the wealthy and powerful.

All these contrasts cause us to feel the alarming distortion of life. Is there no justice? How can God allow this blasphemous inequality? The parable does not answer our questions.

But it does show that the disparities are removed in death. "The poor man died...and the rich man also died" (v. 22). The author of Hebrews echoes the truth: "It is appointed for men to die once and after this comes judgment" (9:27). As the rest of the drama unfolds, we are relieved to learn how the tables are turned in the afterlife. But as different as conditions are for each man, they again share in the universally prescribed appointment not only with death, but also with justice. There is a holiness in the fact that, diverse though their eternal conditions are, they are really only extensions of each man's spiritual condition during life on earth.

Jesus has a word for us in the face of this drastically democratic fact of death and judgment: "Lay up for yourselves treasures in heaven, where neither moth nor rust destroys, and where thieves do not break in or steal; for where your treasure is, there will your heart be also" (Matt. 6:20,21).

Kingdom Thinking

1. What aspect of this parable touched you? What about it made you think?

2. An unbelieving philosopher once warned that

people who spend their lives preparing for life in another world may neglect this one. Do you think he had a point?

3. If the physically dead could communicate with us, what do you think they would say?

4. How do you feel about death? How do you react to the question, "If you were to die physically today, where would you spend eternity?"

Related Readings

Psalm 116:15 Ecclesiastes 12:1-7 1 John 4:16,17

Prayer to the King

We are awed by the certainty of death, dear Lord, but we rejoice in Your promise that we can stand before Your throne of judgment clothed in the blood-washed robes of the Lamb. In view of death, help us not to fail to live every day of our lives. Through Christ our Lord, Amen.

30

A Voice from the Dead

SCRIPTURE READING:

And in Hades he [the rich man] lifted up his eyes, being in torment, and saw Abraham far away, and Lazarus in his bosom. And he cried out and said, "Father Abraham, have mercy on me, and send Lazarus, that he may dip the tip of his finger in water and cool off my tongue; for I am in agony in this flame." But Abraham said, "...between us and you there is a great chasm fixed."

LUKE 16:23-26

The parable of the rich man and Lazarus ushers us into the strange realm of departed spirits. Hebrew beliefs about the afterlife help us to understand. Paradise and

Gehenna were both considered parts of Hades. Paradise was also called "Abraham's bosom," a realm of blessed assurance with the patriarch and all who were experiencing the reward of beatific bliss. Dives is pictured in Gehenna, the name taken from the Valley of Hinnom, the refuse heap outside of Jerusalem that burned but was never consumed.

Our attention is riveted on Dives. He realizes where he is, and that his condition in the eternal fires is irrevocable. Now he has no power to order underlings to satisfy his every whim and desire. The plight of his condition is intensified by his being able to see beyond the wide, yawning gulf between the fires of Gehenna and the glories of paradise. He sees Lazarus reclining in Abraham's bosom. He has no leprous sores on his body; his face no longer has the pallid, tortured look of hunger. Joy radiates about him like a jewel in the sunshine.

Now, he who had thrown bread crumbs out of his window for Lazarus to fight for with the wild dogs wants the liberated leper to cool his fevered tongue! But Abraham's words flash like lightning through Dives' soul. The thought of relief from the burning fire drained his hope that his punishment was temporary. The chasm is "fixed," and "none may cross over from there to us" (Luke 16:26). There is a long silence as the words toll Dives' doom. His soul has never known love, save for a selfish brand of self-gratification. Now, all expectation of release is gone. His anguish is sealed for eternity.

Finally, the corridors of the rich man's mind are occupied by the first selfless thought he has ever entertained. His five brothers! They must be warned about what happens after death (see vv. 27,28). They must be alerted to the fate of those who do not believe, show compassion or prepare for eternity beyond death's decisive door. Again, Abraham's answer is incisive: "If they do not listen to Moses and the Prophets, neither will they be persuaded if someone rises from the dead" (v. 31). Moses had clearly delineated the ethical life, and the prophets had sounded a clarion call for justice, faithfulness and obedience.

The curtain closes slowly on the final act of this drama. What does it all mean? The Lord has drawn aside the thick, mysterious veil between the here and now, and the then and forever. As we meditate on this stirring parable, we realize that we have been given a warning that can become the basis of a vibrant hope. The truths mount in ascending power and resound in our souls.

First, we see clearly that we will all live forever. Immortality is not our choice. Death is not an ending, but a transition in immortal life; it is impotent in its attempt to destroy the inner person. This makes it urgent that we consider the question, Where will we spend eternity?

Second, Jesus has shown that there are two distinct realms of life after death. He proclaimed the Kingdom of heaven, and called people to begin a joyous relationship with God that would go on for eternity. But His teaching about hell was no less vivid. Its undeniable reality is seen, for example, in His stern word to those who were hostile to His message of love: "You serpents, you brood of vipers, how shall you escape the sentence of hell?" (Matt. 23:33).

Third, the parable has taught us that what we do about what we believe determines our eternal destiny. Lazarus did not go to Abraham's bosom because he had been poor, nor Dives to hellfire because he was rich. Their destiny was sealed in their souls long before they died, teaching us that we will continue in eternity in the spiritual condition we have spent the years of our lives on earth.

Finally, the parable teaches us that the demarcation line of death is final. No communication can be possible with those on this side of the grave. There is only one voice from the dead; His name is Jesus. And His word is: "I am the resurrection and the life; he who believes in Me shall live even if he dies" (John 11:25).

Kingdom Thinking

1. Some Christians are quite happy about the prospects of eternal bliss, but are troubled about the

New Testament teaching about eternal torment. How do you feel about this?

2. A person said, "I'm signed, sealed and my destination is heaven!" How do you feel about this statement? Is it too cocky? Or is it an assurance any Christian should be able to express?

3. If the afterlife is an extension of the person you are now, what would you like to change about yourself in this life?

Related Readings

Leviticus 19:31; 20:6 2 Samuel 12:15-23

Prayer to the King

Dear Lord, we pray for the grace to accept the inevitable fact of death. But while we acknowledge our helplessness before it, we praise You for empowering our Lord Jesus to triumph over death, hell and the grave! We glory in His promise that where He is, there we shall be also. In His strong name, Amen.

Part III

Riches in the Lord's Treasury

31

Buried Treasure

SCRIPTURE READING:

The kingdom of heaven is like a treasure hidden in the field, which a man found and hid; and from joy over it he goes and sells all that he has, and buys that field.

MATTHEW 13:44

The theme of the college conference was Ralph Carmichael's winsome confession of complete commitment, "He's Everything to Me." Each evening the collegians would close the day by singing the words that express the unreserved trust of personal faith: "He's everything to me."

As I watched the joyous faces and heard the gusto of the singing, the words affirmed my own longing to have God be everything to me. The days of the conference had been filled with counseling students. They were wrestling with the problems of conflicting loyalties: studies, career plans, dating, marriage, success and self-images. Their burning questions were: How can I put God first in my life? How do you make a full surrender of your life to know and do the will of God? Why is it so difficult to be a true Christian?

The words of the song gave me God's answer for my final message. You can't say, "He's everything to me!" until you can say and believe, "I'm everything to God!"

That's the exciting truth Jesus communicated to His disciples in the parables of the hidden treasure, and in the pearl of great price (to be considered in the next chapter). He had called His inner band of disciples into intimate conversation. To these men who had responded to His message and were His followers, He gave the secret of how to make the kingdom of God everything to them. In the story of the buried treasure, He explained the surpassing value of the Kingdom and the way to enter into the full joy of the reign and rule of God in their lives.

We can feel the emotions of the plowman working the field. It was leased ground, and He had plowed it many times before. Feel the hot sun beating down, the sweat rolling off his brow, the weary hands gripping the slivered plow handles. Sameness, demanding labor, monotony. All at once the plow hit an obstruction. Another rock to be dug out and carried to the side of the field! He got down on his knees and began to dig with his hands. Clump and clod were removed. The hard earth resisted movement.

Suddenly the man's hand broke through and touched the obstruction. Not granite, but the top edge of a chest! The man's heart began to beat faster. Could it be—? He knew that treasures were often hidden in the ground. There were no banks. People resorted to the earth to hide their valuables. When war or calamity drove them off their land, they would bury their treasures, hoping to return to claim them. The plowman dug furiously, remembering the rabbinical "finders keepers" law of the time. Excitement surged through him as he ripped the chest open and beheld the jewels and curios sparkling in the sunlight.

Then a terrible fright jabbed his mind. Had anyone seen him? He carefully covered the chest, replacing the earth so no one would suspect. Then a plan formed in his mind. At all cost, he must make that field his own so the treasure would also be his. Joy gripped him as he liquidated all other assets and bought the field. Nothing was of value in comparison to possessing that treasure!

We are left to ponder the powerful truth Jesus is telling us. Our first response is, "What means that much to us? What would we value this highly? Do God and His kingdom mean that much to us?" Then we remember Jesus' explanation of the parable of the tares of the field in Matthew 13:37,38—how it is He who sows the good seed, and how the field is the world. It dawns on us that Jesus Himself is the leading character in most all of the parables, and that He is the plowman in the parable of the buried treasure. And if that is so, then we ourselves are the treasure!

God had often told Israel that she was a special treasure "among all the peoples, for all the earth is Mine" (Exod. 19:5). Once it dawns on us that we are treasured by God, we will give everything to possess the treasure of the Kingdom. In other words, the Kingdom must enter into us before we can enter into the Kingdom. We can "seek first the Kingdom of God" only after we know that He has sought us and bought us through calvary, loving us with acceptance and forgiveness that knows no boundary.

What stands in our way of selling all, giving all, committing all? Can anything match the value of being God's cherished person? When we realize that we are the treasure for whom Christ died, we will treasure doing His will at all costs!

Kingdom Thinking

1. Did the way you were raised as a child tend to help you think of yourself as "treasured"? What ordinary events can block this understanding, and how can God's love counter such negative influences?

2. What difference would it make in your life if you

thought of yourself as "treasured" by God? How would it affect your relationships? Your discipleship?

3. How does this parable impact the way we share our faith? How can we communicate how much people mean to God?

Related Readings

Matthew 6:25-34 1 Peter 2:4-10

Prayer to the King

O God, help us not to fall into the trap of false humility, so that we forget we are precious in Your sight. Help us to so value ourselves that we also value the standard of living You desire to see in the people for whom Your Son gave His life. In His name we pray, Amen.

32

You Are the Pearl!

SCRIPTURE READING:

Again, the kingdom of heaven is like a merchant seeking fine pearls, and upon finding one pearl of great value, he went and sold all that he had, and bought it.

MATTHEW 13:45,46

Having captured our attention by the parable of the buried treasure, Jesus goes on to tell another parable with the same point but with its own distinctive elements, drawing us into the drama of a merchant's search for valued pearls.

The man knew pearls. He had spent his life studying them, bartering one for another, upgrading his collection as he traveled from village to village. He had heard of *the* pearl, one of unsurpassed perfection and beauty. We wonder if it was the one that had been the cherished possession of Cleopatra, valued at more than four hundred thousand dollars in our money. The merchant thought of little else. His every conversation focused on it, hoping to glean some new information on where he could find it.

And then one day, there it was! When he saw it, he knew his relentless search was worth the tireless energy. The cost? Name the price! The man had to possess the pearl! He could not contain the joy he felt. Everything he had—possessions, other pearls, life itself—was more than worth the cost. We can empathize with the ecstasy he felt when he finally possessed the pearl of great price. "It's mine! It cost me everything, but it's mine!"

The metaphor of the pearl is drenched with meaning. What do we know about pearls? What would we value as highly as the fine one discovered by the merchant?

Pearls are the result of invasion and injury. They are products of a living organism. A grain of sand gets within the oyster and injures it. The oyster then covers over the injury with nacre or mother-of-pearl, layer upon layer, until the pearl is fashioned. The wounding has become a source of wonder.

The word "pearl" is used only once in the Old Testament. Job said, "The price of wisdom is above pearls" (Job 28:18, *RSV*). But it was not one of the significant words or symbols of Israel. Why then did Jesus speak of a pearl of great price? I believe He carefully selected this metaphor with the metamorphosis of the pearl in mind. The kingdom of God would not be fulfilled without the terrible wounding of calvary. Jesus knew what was ahead for Him; Isaiah had made that clear. The Messiah would be "wounded for our transgressions." And yet, from Golgotha's wounds the world would be won.

Only the power of love can make us realize how much we mean to God. Our self-deprecation debilitates us. Life's blows form negative self-images and lack of self-esteem. How can we accept the love God offers? We are not worth the Incarnation; we have done nothing to deserve such a love. The Lord knows the injury and the wounds of our experiences. And He uses them to make a pearl. The magnificent metaphor is twofold: what Christ means to us, and what we mean to Him.

The point is this: You and I are central in the strategy of the Kingdom. The rule of God must begin within us, then reside among us, and eventually pervade all areas of life. God has elected us to be the channels of His plan and purpose in the world. Once we realize that in God's calculus we are pearls without peer, we in turn will "sell" all we have to obtain the pearl of great price for us—knowing and serving Him.

So often the gospel is preached or taught in the

grim ambience of what we must give up before we can realize God's grace. That is backward. What God has done for us is the only adequate motivation for what we are to do and be in response. Once we catch a glimpse of the extent of His love, we will respond with passionate purpose as did the merchant who sold all he had to purchase the pearl.

The apostle Paul experienced the gospel in this way, for he could say, "I count all things to be loss in view of the surpassing value of knowing Christ Jesus my Lord, for whom I have suffered the loss of all things, and count them but rubbish in order that I may gain Christ...that I may know Him, and the power of His resurrection" (Phil. 3:8-10). The value of the pearl of great value makes all our worthy ambitions secondary to our ultimate purpose. The lesser pearls of our pleasures, plans, priorities and popularity must be surrendered to claim the pearl of God's absolute rule in all of life's relationships and responsibilities.

Kingdom Thinking

1. Have you ever experienced a loss or other painful "invasion" in your life, comparable to a grain of sand in an oyster, that eventually resulted in a blessing you wouldn't have known otherwise?

2. Carry Jesus' metaphor of the pearl of great value further: What healing influences does God often send

to act as "mother-of-pearl," building up valuable layers of healing in a wounded life?

3. In your experience, has the gospel been preached "backward," leaving the impression that if we will just become valuable, Jesus will love us?

4. From your own experience, what difference does it make to think of yourself as a valued pearl? Conversely, how does that affect our attitude about knowing and serving Christ as the pearl of great value?

Related Readings

Romans 5:1-8 1 Corinthians 10:13 Ephesians 2:1-10

Prayer to the King

How grateful we are that You have found us and bought us, O Lord! In return, help us see You in all Your beauty, and to allow nothing and no one to gain greater priority. In the name of Him who gave His all to redeem us, Amen.

33

Negative Neutrality

SCRIPTURE READING:

Then some of the scribes and Pharisees answered Him, saying, "Teacher, we want to see a sign from You." But He answered and said to them, "An evil and adulterous generation craves for a sign; and yet no sign shall be given to it but the sign of Jonah the prophet; for just as Jonah was three days and three nights in the belly of the sea monster, so shall the Son of Man be three days and three nights in the heart of the earth."

MATTHEW 12:38-40

The scene with the scribes and the Pharisees will lead to Jesus' parable of the empty house (see Matt. 12:43-45), whose specifics will occupy us in the next chapter. But, first, we should notice carefully how Jesus builds up to the figure of an empty house by showing how desperately empty are the hearts of His enemies. They make a show of neutrality or objectivity by asking for a sign. But Jesus knows that their hearts are simply vacant, not neutral. And He contrasts their brand of skepticism with three Old Testament cases of doubters who were more open to being moved to faith.

The only sign for these skeptics was that of the prophet Jonah (see vv. 39,40). Our minds scurry back to the reluctant prophet who ran away to sea because his faith was too weak to preach to the Ninevites. We recall that when the boatmen cast Jonah overboard to save themselves from the violent storm, the prophet was swallowed by a great fish. He was cast up on the shore three days later—just as Jesus would be in the tomb for three days before being raised from the dead. It was a "conversion experience" for Jonah! He obediently preached to the wicked city of Nineveh—no miracles or divinations, just clear preaching of God's sovereignty over all creation. And they repented!

The Ninevites are the second case of a people whose hearts were not merely neutral but hardened. But Jesus drives home the point that the wicked, Gentile Ninevites had hearts that were more open to God's message than were Jesus' own detractors, even though their preacher was a lesser prophet than Jesus (see v. 41).

While the Pharisees contemplate this disturbing thrust, Jesus adds the story of the Queen of Sheba from Solomon's days. She came to Jerusalem saying, "I did not believe the reports" (1 Kings 10:7) of Solomon's wealth and wisdom—again not simply neutral, but skeptical. Yet, she went away confessing that "the half was not told me." But even though a "greater than Solomon" confronted these scribes and Pharisees, they stood judged in their unbelief by "the Queen of the South" (Matt. 12:42).

Who but the Messiah could have greater wisdom than Solomon? Exactly! The only sign Jesus gives His opponents is that of Himself. For those willing to cleanse their hearts of negative presuppositions and calculated unbelief, that should be enough. But the scribes and Pharisees had come with a studied attempt at neutrality that belied the ugliness in their hearts. Their feigned objectivity actually had become a guise for active resistance.

The fact is, the scribes and Pharisees' "neutral" hearts could not become the containers and communicators of the Holy Spirit as God intended. Jesus came to be "God with us," creating a new breed of people in whom He could live. Messiah had come to these religious leaders: "He came to His own, and those who were His own did not receive Him" (John 1:11). Neutrality was their nemesis.

So Jesus turned to the common people to create a new Israel. And they heard Him gladly, responding not with neutrality but with positive and ready receptivity. "But as many as received Him, to them He gave the right to become children of God, even to those who believe in His name, who were born not of blood, nor of the will of the flesh, nor of the will of man, but of God" (John 1:12,13).

Pentecost became the triumphant climax of the Incarnation. As the Spirit of God had dwelt in Jesus, now through His death and resurrection the original purpose of creation had been reclaimed. The empty—but *receptive*—hearts of the apostles were filled with the Holy Spirit. God had made His home in them. Each new challenge brought fresh infilling in the remarkable lives we see spread across the pages of the book of Acts.

This is the positive side of what seems to be a negative introduction to the parable to follow. True openness does not require indisputable signs in order to believe. Instead, it prepares a dwelling place for God's Holy Spirit.

Kingdom Thinking

1. What is the one most compelling reason you are a believer?

2. Do you sometimes think your faith would be stronger if you saw more signs of the reality of God, Christ or the Holy Spirit? What kind of signs would they be? Could any sign really convince a heart that is totally neutral about believing?

3. Sometimes even the hearts of believers feel "empty." Does this ever happen to you? Can you identify the cause? What do you do during such times?

Related Readings

1 Kings 10:1-7 John 20:24-29 1 Corinthians 1:22-25

Prayer to the King

Dear Lord, we believe—help Thou our unbelief! Give us hearts that are disposed to faith, and souls that are ready dwellings for Your Spirit. Help us to believe when we cannot see, to obey when we cannot understand, to follow when we do not know where You are leading. Through Christ our Lord, Amen.

34

Satan Abhors a Vacuum, Too

SCRIPTURE READING:

Now when the unclean spirit goes out of a man, it passes through waterless places, seeking rest, and does not find it. Then it says, "I will return to my house from which I came"; and when it comes, it finds it unoccupied, swept, and put in order. Then it goes, and takes along with it seven other spirits more wicked than itself, and they go in and live there.

MATTHEW 12:43-45

I am convinced that Jesus' parable of the empty house was an anticipation of the fulfillment of His life and ministry as well as a reflection of what He observed in

His people. He came not only to extricate people's hearts from Satan's grip, but also to fill them with the Holy Spirit. We were meant to be the dwelling place of God. He is the tenant who owns the house.

The parable teaches us the danger of the emptiness of negative virtue. Reformation without regeneration leaves us in the same condition as the empty house. Often, we are similar to the rulers who resisted Jesus: We have done our best to cleanse our lives of the habits, thoughts and patterns that would not be pleasing to God, but we often know more about what we are against than what we are for. We have a multiplicity of don'ts, but little power to do.

Is this too harsh? Perhaps. But how else can we explain the lack of warmth and joy among so many Christians? For many, God is a cosmic truant officer instead of the tenant who owns the house. Has our religion released us to be life-affirming, contagious, enabling lovers of people? Do we find it difficult to be Christians in life's pressures and demands? I wonder if we have done well at cleansing the house; but it still stands empty, open for the restless demons—now sevenfold—to take possession.

Surely, this must be the explanation of the checkered history of Christianity. We can understand how people who call themselves Christians do the dreadful things they do—often in the name of Christ. Satan has occupied the house!

And why is it that personal and social advancement must so often climb over the stiffened backs of Christians? Can Satan twist our thinking, distort our vision and cripple our effectiveness? He not only can, but, he also does! Whenever we have evicted the Holy Spirit's rule and guidance, we can be sure that the emptiness will be replaced with seven demons: pride, selfishness, false ambition, competition, willfulness, distrust and arrogance. They are always outside an empty heart, waiting to repossess us. Our only protection is consistent communion with Christ, and daily infilling of the Holy Spirit.

This explains the dynamics of the Spirit-filled life of the man called Saul of Tarsus. After casting out his demons of unbelief, the Spirit transformed Saul into a Spirit-filled apostle who did more than any other Christian in history to put into writing the distilled essence of God's original purpose for His people. Where would we be if Saul had remained as he had been—empty, void of God's Holy Spirit?

An active, positive life of living what we believe, and communicating it to others is the surest way to keep our Christianity alive. We will lose what we do not use. The only way to overcome a bad habit is by starting a creative one. The safeguard against losing our Christianity is giving it away. As long as our society is filled with injustice, prejudice, greed and dehumanization, our work is not finished. Unless we are engaged in changing the world, the world will change us. And our last condition will be worse than the first, before we met Christ. Why? Because then two masters will reside in the same house. And we can only serve one master.

The parable of the empty house presses us on to grow. Christianity is more than rearranging the status quo or repositioning the cherished furniture of the past in our hearts. Paul was vividly clear: "If any man is in Christ, he is a new creature; the old things passed away; behold, new things have come" (2 Cor. 5:17). Be sure the new has come into the house, or it won't be long before the old will fill up the vacuum.

On the last night of His ministry, before He was crucified, Jesus unveiled the liberating secret of how the empty house was to be filled. "If anyone loves Me, he will keep My word; and My Father will love him, and We will come to him, and make Our abode with Him" (John 14:23).

Kingdom Thinking

1. What does this parable and the explanation of this chapter mean to you personally?

2. Has the emphasis in contemporary Christianity, as you have known it, been more on *cleansing* the house, or on *filling* it with the Holy Spirit?

3. How does this parable apply to overcoming

bad attitudes and habits? Considering all kinds of uncreative mental and physical addictions, reflect on 1 Corinthians 6:19,20. On a daily basis, do you think of your life as your own, or as belonging to Christ and filled with the Holy Spirit? Why is this sometimes difficult to remember?

Related Readings

Philippians 4:4-9 Colossians 2:20-23 2 Peter 1:5-11

Prayer to the King

Dear Lord, we sometimes seem so conditioned to expect religion to tell us no, that we cannot hear it when faith tells us yes. Help us to model our lives after the Christ who loved people, lived life to the fullest and promised to fill the houses of our hearts with the joy of the Holy Spirit. In His name we pray, Amen.

35

How to Attend a Banquet

Scripture Reading:

When you give a reception, invite the poor, the crippled, the lame, the blind, and you will be blessed, since they do not have the means to repay you; for you will be repaid at the resurrection of the righteous. And when one of those who were reclining at the table with Him heard this, he said to Him, "Blessed is everyone who shall eat bread in the kingdom of God!"

Luke 14:13-15

Not long ago, my family was having a very special celebration. A piercing question from one of my sons suddenly shocked me into realizing that I had drifted off into private thought. "Hey Dad!" he said. "Where are you?"

It should have been obvious where I was. I was seated at the head of my dining room table and taking part in the celebration. But my son realized that even though I was present physically, my attention was elsewhere. A pressing problem I had on my mind when I came home had captured my attention. I was not "tending to" the party with my full presence, thought or emotional investment.

Jesus had been invited to a party, too (see Luke 14:1). The invitation to attend a banquet at the home of a leading Pharisee was very significant to Him. Only the day before, He had symbolized the messianic age by describing it as a joyous banquet: "And they will come from east and west, and from north and south, and will recline at the table in the kingdom of God" (Luke 13:29). For Jesus, the long-awaited age had come. No banquet, especially among the leaders of His people, could be attended without the deeper meaning reverberating in His heart.

From the moment we enter the banquet hall with the Master, we realize that the Pharisees are not "attending" the banquet as Jesus was. They are present, but not really *present*. They watch Him closely. His every word and movement are being scrutinized. The air is hostile and competitive. This cannot be a messianic banquet for them, for they do not acknowledge that the Messiah is present. They have other things on their minds.

For one thing, who would be given the seats of honor? Everyone seems to be maneuvering for the seats closest to the host. Some brush by the Master in a frantic effort to be recognized and honored. Then, when the scramble for the best seats is finally over, a shocking thing happens. All eyes turn to Jesus, as a man suffering from dropsy makes his way across the banquet hall and stands before Him. Everyone seems impatient with the interruption of the intruder—except the Messiah. They watch to see whether He would break the law and tend to the man on the Sabbath.

When power surges through Jesus' divine hands and the man is healed, it should have been enough to justify the messianic claims that had prompted the banquet. But the Pharisees are so concerned about the rules of Sabbath-keeping that they cannot "come to the party" and celebrate with the man who is made whole.

Then, a Pharisee at the banquet interrupts the Master by blurting out a kind of slogan that had become trite by repetition, even though it had a messianic ring to it. With pomp and ceremony the man says, "Blessed is everyone who shall eat bread in the kingdom of God!" (v. 15). It is as if he had said, "Won't it be wonderful to eat bread with the Messiah when He comes!" What he does not recognize is that the Messiah has already come. He is present at that very banquet he is attending.

The question my son asked of me, "Hey, where are

you?" could well be asked of the Pharisees, and of all of us. We can miss the great things God is doing and and revealing all around us. It's possible to be in church and miss out on the fellowship we should enjoy there. We can hear the magnificent truths of the gospel and not experience them. God's gifts of people can be offered, only to find us not awake to the unique expression of God's love that He has wrapped up in human personality just for us. The natural world around us can sing its doxology of praise to the Creator, but we do not hear. God can write His signature in the amazing surprises of His grace, but we cannot see it.

The messianic age is now. We are the Messiah's people. The banquet table is teeming with the blessings of love, forgiveness, indwelling power and unlimited hope.

While at the banquet, attend to the banquet!

Kingdom Thinking

1. Think for a moment of the *people* in your life who mean the most to you. Name some ways they enrich your life, but that you sometimes overlook or take for granted.

2. In a similar way, think of some recent *events* in your life, or even in the daily news, that reveal godly love or a "Kingdom moment" if we but "attend" to it carefully.

3. What are some factors or influences that often blind us to the presence of Christ and His kingdom among us?

4. What are some ways God's people can encourage each other to discern this presence more often?

Related Readings

Luke 24:13-16,28-35 Romans 10:6-10

Prayer to the King

The world is too much with us, dear Father! Help us to see Your love in our loved ones, Your kingdom in acts of compassion, Your grace in life itself. We affirm that the Messiah is among us; help us to experience the joy of being in His presence. Through Jesus Christ our Lord, Amen.

36

No Time for a Party?

SCRIPTURE READING:

A certain man was giving a big dinner, and he invited many; and at the dinner hour he sent his slave to say to those who had been invited, "Come; for everything is ready now." But they all alike began to make excuses....And the master said to the slave, "Go out into the highways and along the hedges, and compel them to come in, that my house may be filled. For I tell you, none of those men who were invited shall taste of my dinner."

LUKE 14:16-18,23,24

The "certain man" in Luke 14:16 is God. The preparation of the ages had preceded the coming of Jesus, the

Messiah. For centuries, He had worked out His purposes in history to bring humankind to this moment. He had sent Christ to live among His people. Now the messianic banquet was prepared. It was time to celebrate!

We are amazed to read in verses 18-20 the flimsy excuses for not attending the great feast. We feel the anguish of Jesus' experience of rejection by the leaders of His own people. A great deal has been made of the various excuses they make for not being able to attend His great feast. The main point, however, is that any excuse would be offered at all! The invitations had been sent out long before the event, and the parable implies that they had been accepted. When the time of the banquet arrived, and the invited guests were reminded of their commitment, they sent superficial excuses to the host. Each excuse is incongruous and absurd.

Who would buy a field without going to see it first? Land was very valuable in Jesus' day, and the purchase of property was a serious matter. Only the most affluent could delegate the negotiation for acquisition of land. And even if the man had bought property, going to see it was not a good reason for breaking a previous promise. The man had a deeper reason for refusing to go. He was distracted by his material possessions.

The second man's excuse was no more believable. Five yoke of oxen, ten oxen, indicated great wealth. It would be very unusual for anyone affluent enough to buy ten oxen to try them out himself—he would have his servants do that. No one would buy oxen without first being sure they were sound. If oxen were the man's hobby and he wanted to see how they would work the field, he could find another time to do that. The truth was that he didn't want to go to the banquet. The flimsy excuse was an affront.

The last man's evasion was ludicrous. Deuteronomy 24:5 gave him scriptural justification for his excuse. For a whole year after being married, a man was relieved of duties and responsibilities usually required of him. He did not have to go to meetings or to war. But, again, the excuse was a smoke screen. The man used a legality to justify his absence. Beneath it was the true reason: He didn't want to go.

Jesus is telling us that the people's longing for the Messiah was not authentic. And in telling us this, He has drawn us into the parable. We find ourselves in those three reluctant guests. Do we really want the kingdom of God if it means the absolute rule of the Lord in our lives? We talk a great deal about our need for Christ in our lives. How much do we want Him? Why are we so quick to make excuses when He invades our lives and wants to take charge of our minds and hearts? Is it possible that we want our relationship with Him on our own terms? What's the real reason we stay away from the feast?

The end of this parable is very significant. Jesus

tells us plainly that God will bypass people who equivocate. Yet, His banquet hall will be filled—with people who recognize their need and desire to be with Him. Did the Pharisees know what Jesus was implying? They were the invited guests who refused to come to the banquet. Are we refusing? Our excuses echo in our souls. We have been confronted by the graciousness and the severity of God. He invites us again and again, and we decline. A time will come when our persistent refusals will fire His indignation. This leads us to an honest facing of why we trifle with the Almighty God.

Now, we can understand the urgent implications of the parable of the great feast. It focuses God's loving preparation for the messianic banquet, and His gracious invitation to us. The invitations have gone out, written in the blood of calvary. Will we come?

Kingdom Thinking

1. In what ways does the material world often come between Christians and their wholehearted acceptance of Jesus' invitation to establish His rule in their hearts?

2. What special problems did the Pharisees have that contributed to their general rejection of Jesus as the Messiah? (See, for example, Matt. 15:3-6; 23:23.)

3. What other distractions keep many modern people from giving God first place in their hearts?

Related Readings

Luke 6:46-49 Luke 7:31-35 Revelation 19:7-10

Prayer to the King

Lord, in the midst of our busy lives and the bustle of daily concerns, we hear Your loving invitation. Grant that we might treasure the privilege of coming to Your table over all distractions, all other needs. Help us to be honest in our desire to make You Lord of our lives. In the name of Jesus we pray, Amen.

37

The God of the Successful

SCRIPTURE READING:

The land of a certain rich man was very productive. And he began reasoning to himself, saying, "What shall I do, since I have no place to store my crops?" And he said, "This is what I will do: I will tear down my barns and build larger ones, and there I will store all my grain and my goods."

LUKE 12:16-18

The title of this chapter may have alarmed you. "The God of the successful"? What do we mean by that? Is God only concerned about successful people? What about failures? Isn't the Bible filled with accounts of what God did with failures in spite of their inadequacies? Yes, but what would you call what they accomplished when they allowed God to love and use them? Would you call that success?

Success has become a dirty word in some Christian circles. We look down our noses at successful people. Often when describing what a person was before conversion we allude to his worldly success as if the new life in Christ will now make him a worldly loser.

Is the Lord against success? Doesn't He want us to use our gifts, multiply our resources and maximize our opportunities? Why are we critical of successful people? What is this love-hate implication we give when we condemn prosperity all through the year, then go to the prosperous at stewardship time to collect the results of their industry? We honor successful entertainers and leaders, and at the same time give the impression that if they really loved Jesus they would sell all and go into the professional ministry. Is anything wrong with being successful?

We must define our terms. Success is the favorable or prosperous course or accomplishment of anything attempted. The word "success" implies the result or outcome of a plan, purpose or effort. A successful person is one who obtains what he desires or intends. He accomplishes what he sets out to do. Nothing is wrong with fulfilling a purpose or accomplishing a goal. The crucial issue is the nature of the desired end; true success is measured by that.

The question is, Who is the God of the successful? The G may be upper or lowercase. It is possible to create a god of our own, making and building our ideas of success around that idol. We can deify our ideas of prosperity and miss the relationship with the true God. The Lord God who is Creator, Sustainer and Redeemer of the world, does want us to be successful—but according to His goals, plan and design. The authentically successful have Him and His will as the measurement of their success.

The rich man of the parable we are considering was successful by some standards. He had accomplished what he set out to do—and more. But he had missed the purpose of his life. His voice of assurance came from within himself, an echo of his own frenzied accumulation. The voice of God interrupted his self-accolade: "You fool! This very night your soul is required of you; and now who will own what you have prepared?" (Luke 12:20).

The Greek word for soul used here is *psyche*. It refers to the mental capacity. The rich fool was really saying, "Just think, my mental plans will be achieved. What I thought to be important will be accomplished." Driving such mental images is a hard god to satisfy. If possessions are our mental goal, they will eventually possess us. Materialism is a hungry suckling—never satisfied.

What we think about ourselves, life and our purpose forms our destiny. An old saying states, "You can't take it with you." Not true! We will take what our thoughts have determined us to become. We all live forever; the question is how, where and with whom. Devoid of our physical body and the material possessions that have insulated us from reality, the inner person will live in communion with God or without Him. The "wealth addict" has nothing to take with him except the miserable person he has shaped in the image of his god.

Success, then, is cooperating with God in establishing His kingdom in our hearts, our affairs, our personal relationships and our society. Whatever else we accomplish during the years of life, however much we accumulate or acquire, unless we discover a personal relationship with Christ, seek to do His will in all of life and test everything according to His purpose, we will not be successful.

Right at this moment, God wants to make you successful—on His terms, by His power and in His timing. He is the God of the successful.

Kingdom Thinking

1. Make a list of several standards of success in your own mind. If material wealth is one of them, be honest enough to include it in your list. Where do healthy human relationships come on the list? Relationship with God?

2. Evaluate the common line, "Money isn't everything, but it's way ahead of whatever is in second place."

3. Describe someone you know who is both materially and spiritually successful.

Related Readings

Proverbs 11:24-28 Ecclesiastes 5:10-20
Matthew 6:19-21

Prayer to the King

Help us, O Lord, to have no other gods before You—neither riches nor glory nor others nor the desire to be liked by other people. Grant that we might value spiritual riches over the material, and give You first place in our hearts.
In Jesus' name, Amen.

38

The Perpendicular Pronoun

SCRIPTURE READING:

And I will say to my soul, "Soul, you have many goods laid up for many years to come; take your ease, eat, drink and be merry." But God said to him, "You fool! This very night your soul is required of you; and now who will own what you have prepared?" So is the man who lays up treasure for himself, and is not rich toward God.

LUKE 12:19-21

The pronouns used in the parable of the rich fool expose the wrong kind of success. In Luke 12:17-19, "I" is used six times; "my" is used five times, with a self-gratifying "you" referring to the rich man himself, thrown in for good measure. The man's whole life was inverted on himself.

He "began reasoning to himself" (v. 17). He talked to the wrong person. His dialogue with himself was circular refortification of his self-image and presuppositions. No one else was consulted for perspective, least of all God. His goal to achieve ease, and to eat, drink and be merry was the measurement of his success. His decisions about what to do with his multiplied prosperity all had to fit that purpose. The possessive of the perpendicular pronoun "I" possessed him: my crops, my grain, my barns, my soul. The last was the fatal assumption. He talked to his own soul to get the answer he wanted about how to support his addiction to the habit-forming narcotic of materialism.

Jesus adds His startling commentary to the story: "So is the man who lays up treasure for himself, and is not rich toward God" (v. 21). Eternal life is richness toward God. Anything that keeps us from being rich with God now will debilitate our eternal life with Him forever after our physical death. Therefore, we are urgently pressed to consider what richness toward God is about. The sharp focus of Jesus' message is that our spiritual wealth is inherited, not earned. A free gift is offered. Richness with God begins in a relationship with Him through Christ. Love and forgiveness are given without measure. Christ died and rose again to reconcile us with

God. Life begins anew. Companionship with God Himself is given to us.

Our richness toward God grows as we surrender the direction, goals and purposes of our lives to seek first the kingdom of God. The passion of our lives becomes seeking and doing the will of God.

Inadvertently, we begin to grow in Christlikeness. Paul spoke of the riches of the glory of the mystery of Christ in us, the hope of glory (see Col. 1:27). From within, our mental disposition about life is reformed around the Lord's goals and strategy.

Daily, and hour by hour, God guides us as we share in His work. We begin to realize that all our opportunities are given for a purpose. Every person and situation is an occasion for us to cooperate with what God wants to accomplish.

A part of being rich toward God includes people and society—being able to share hope with others by introducing them to the new life in Christ. This requires listening, showing love, identifying and being involved. The more we give away our spiritual wealth, the more it grows and the more it means to us. Concern for people can never be separated from caring about the practical needs of their lives. God has entrusted resources to us to meet the physical, emotional and spiritual needs of people. Even material wealth can make us rich toward God—if it is shared with others!

Richness toward God develops as we allow Him to use us in areas of the responsibility He has entrusted to us. Each of us has influence. We are where we are, have the power we have and are able to accomplish what we do because of the providence of God. It's when we say, "Lord, I have achieved nothing without Your grace!" that we are able to ask Him to use us to claim the arena of our responsibilities. Our homes, churches, schools, jobs, neighborhoods and communities belong to Him. He has placed us in them to live out the implications of radical obedience. He wants us to succeed there. The Lord is on the move in society and He wants us to join Him.

By having this understanding of richness, we can confront the troublesome problem of riches. Anytime the acquiring, saving, parlaying or inordinate preoccupation with wealth keep us from richness toward God, it is not only wrong, but also dangerous. It has the possibility of causing us to miss the purpose of life.

As for the rich fool, his overuse of the perpendicular pronoun was his downfall. He began by talking to himself, and he wound up with no one to blame but himself.

Kingdom Thinking

1. Why is it so hard to think of what we have as belonging to God? What causes the change from "His" to "mine"?

2. Is it possible for middle-class people to be as preoccupied with themselves and with things as the rich? Why?

3. Think about what the term "wealthy" means. How much money would you need to consider yourself wealthy? When does wealth cripple our discipleship?

4. How does tithing help to keep our thinking straight?

Related Readings

1 Timothy 6:6-10   Hebrews 13:5   James 2:1-9

Prayer to the King

Dear Father, like the world, the self is too much with us. We cannot even pray to You without being aware of ourselves, of our own neediness before You. Grant that we may fix our eyes on Your Son to draw ourselves out of our selves, and to devote ourselves to serving You, and to meeting the needs of others. Through Christ we pray, Amen.

39

Prepared by the Spirit

SCRIPTURE READING:

Then the kingdom of heaven will be comparable to ten virgins, who took their lamps, and went out to meet the bridegroom. And five of them were foolish, and five were prudent. For when the foolish took their lamps, they took no oil with them, but the prudent took oil in flasks along with their lamps.

MATTHEW 25:1-4

The parable of the bridesmaids is a parable of sheer joy. Weddings were a time of joyous celebration. The festivities lasted a whole week. Regular duties and religious obligations were dispensed with by law so the wedding party and all the guests could relish the full delight of the occasion.

The high point of the week of celebration was when the bridegroom came to the bride's home to take her to their new home. Great pageantry and drama had become a part of the tradition surrounding this event. The bride would ask ten of her friends to be bridesmaids. Their special task was to be part of the processional from her parents' house to her new home. Usually this took place at night, so the major responsibility of the bridesmaids was to carry lamps to light the joyous way of the wedding party. The time when the bridegroom would come was kept a secret. It was to be a surprise, and the bride and her bridesmaids were to be waiting expectantly.

In Jesus' parable, five prudent bridesmaids had brought extra oil for the wait. Five others, however, foolishly went unprepared. As the hours went by, the lamps carried by these attendants began to flicker and then go out. They could not share in the wedding celebration. They missed the joy!

Jesus told this parable in response to the disciples' frightened questions about the future. When would the Lord return? The parable of the bridesmaids was intended to teach them to be prepared whether His coming was soon or late. Jesus is of course the Bridegroom, and His people are the waiting attendants. But what meaning should we assign to the oil?

I believe we can view it as standing for the Holy Spirit, that indwelling, anointing Power that produces bright, radiant, expectant Christians. The oil of the Spirit prepares us with expectancy and anticipation for the breakthrough of the Lord's coming in each day's experiences. Christians who are filled with the Spirit wait upon the Lord, long for His interventions, expect them and are ready for them in the complexities and confusion of life. They are constantly on the lookout, asking, "What is the Lord saying to me in this? What is He trying to teach me in this problem? How will He come into this opportunity and enable me to grasp its full potential?"

Being filled with the Holy Spirit makes us ready-for-anything Christians. We can say, "Let life happen! Let it come with winter winds and its disappointments, its springtime of unanticipated delight, its arduous days and restless nights. We are ready! We are open to grow, agile to regroup, free to fail, willing to cut our losses and able to surge ahead."

It may sound redundant, but it's true: preparation to receive the Bridegroom is provided by the Bridegroom. The Lord who taught this startling parable rose from the dead, returned as reigning Lord and poured out the power of the Holy Spirit. He is the third Person of the Trinity, who existed with the Father and the Son before Creation and time began. He was present at Creation, active all through Israel's history, and directly involved in the birth, ministry, death and resurrection of Christ. Now His role is to glorify Christ and to enable us to love and serve Him.

The Holy Spirit's ministry is to teach us all that Jesus said and did—to make the gospel real and irresistible. From within us, in our hearts, the Holy Spirit gives the gift of faith to accept what God has done for us in Christ, and then to make us expectant of the Lord's interventions in our daily lives. Make no mistake: The Holy Spirit prepares us for what the Lord has prepared for us!

Some interpretations of this parable are grim and focused on judgment. Certainly, there is a solemn warning here against being unprepared, as we shall see. But thinking of the oil of preparedness as the Holy Spirit strikes a joyful note in the parable. After all, "joy" is one of the fruits of the Spirit! (see Gal. 5:22). In this light, the old folk tune articulates the appropriate prayer: "Give me oil in my lamp, keep me burning. Give me oil in my lamp, I pray. Give me oil in my lamp, keep me burning. Keep me burning till the break of day!"

Kingdom Thinking

1. What has been your experience with the Holy Spirit? Does the idea of His indwelling make you think of losing control, or do you view Him as a positive, guiding presence and a source of joy?

2. What would you do to prepare for Christ's second coming if you knew it would occur tomorrow?

3. If the lamp oil in this parable represents the Holy Spirit, what is the implication of the five foolish bridesmaids' allowing it to run out? What can we do to keep our "lamps" replenished with the Spirit? (See Luke 11:13; note that Paul's admonition, "Be filled with the Spirit" [Eph. 5:18], is in the present passive imperative, and should be translated, "Keep on being filled with the Spirit.")

Related Readings

1 Thessalonians 5:1-11 2 Peter 3:1-9 2 Peter 3:10-18

Prayer to the King

We look forward eagerly to Your coming again, Lord Jesus. And while we anticipate that great day, help us to live in the joy of the Spirit, with lighted lamps, redeeming the time, ministering to others, growing in Your grace and knowledge, and expectant for Your daily interventions and serendipities. In Your name, Amen.

40

We Can't Borrow Preparedness

SCRIPTURE READING:

Now while the bridegroom was delaying, they all got drowsy and began to sleep. But at midnight there was a shout, "Behold, the bridegroom! Come out to meet him." Then all those virgins arose, and trimmed their lamps. And the foolish said to the prudent, "Give us some of your oil, for our lamps are going out." But the prudent answered, saying, "No, there will not be enough for us and you too; go instead to the dealers and buy some for yourselves."

MATTHEW 25:5-9

A chicory coffee concentrate from Scotland provides a

delightful bit of memory of my student days in Edinburgh. The label shows a picture of a kilted Scot regiment guard. The motto of the regiment is printed above the imposing, armed, prepared-for-battle highlander: "Ready, Aye, Ready!" The phrase usually sparks some interesting breakfast conversation at our house about the challenges of the day ahead. Often, when my wife asks me how I am and what's anticipated in the day before me, I put on a thick, studied Scottish burr and chant with gusto, "Ready, aye, ready!"

Jesus built the parable of the bridesmaids with dramatic skill. The ten attendants waited patiently for the bridegroom. Soon the exhaustion of the exciting festivities, coupled with the long wait, made them sleepy. One of the things a bridegroom would try to do was to catch the bridal party napping. He was required by custom to send a courier ahead of him, shouting, "Behold, the bridegroom! Come out to meet him." Sure enough, the courier found that all ten bridesmaids had fallen asleep, and their lamps had flickered out.

The lamps were wooden staffs with a dish on top in which was placed a piece of rope or wick dipped in oil. Extra oil was usually carried to replenish the oil in the dish. It's the lack of that extra supply that exposes the folly of the foolish bridesmaids. Their urgent request was for a portion of the supply brought along by the wise, prudent bridesmaids. They refused. Their supply was just enough for themselves. There was nothing for the unprepared bridesmaids to do but rush off to purchase more oil—and, thus, they missed the wedding procession.

Before we charge the five prudent bridesmaids with being selfish and insensitive, we should remember that if they gave their reserve oil to the foolish, unprepared attendants, all ten lamps would go out before the night's task was complete. Their refusal stabs us awake with one of the truths Jesus wanted to drive home with this parable: *We cannot borrow preparedness*.

Jesus wanted His listeners to grapple with this issue. Why do we run out of power and light today? Do we think we can borrow preparedness for life's crises from others? Being prepared requires being filled with the power of the Holy Spirit—and no one can do this for us. Without Him, our lamps will go out. The time to get ready is before, not during, the demanding moment. If we are ready, we can take it!

Shakespeare expressed this clearly:

> There is a tide in the affairs of men
> Which, taken at the flood, leads on to
> fortune.
> Omitted, all the voyage of their life
> Is bound in shallows and in miseries
> On such a full sea are we now afloat
> And we must take the current when it
> serves
> Or lose our ventures.[1]

So many of us lose our ventures, miss our God-appointed opportunity, because we are unprepared to see and grasp the moment. The Holy Spirit helps us discern what is primary and crucial. He gives us the gift of wisdom to see the Lord's approach and to open ourselves to be participants in His strategy.

To be "ready, aye, ready" for life's surprises is demanding. It means being in good spiritual condition and having our prayer muscles well exercised. Perhaps this is why some Christians are more effective and useful than others. We try to explain it by saying that they have unusual talents and spectacular gifts. It may well be that they are simply more exercised in readiness. The Lord is constantly looking for willing, cooperative, daring people who will believe that nothing is impossible for Him. Most of us live with second, third or fourth best because we are unprepared for the propitious moment when the Lord calls.

The life of saints is not just marked by great deeds performed by human skill, but by being prepared for God's intervening miracle. We cannot prepare for a crisis during a crisis!

Kingdom Thinking

1. How is attempting to borrow spiritual preparedness different from borrowing money from the bank?
2. What daily disciplines of the spiritual life might

gradually build up the strength of preparedness for larger battles?

3. Does affirming our need to be prepared within ourselves mean that we can't draw strength and inspiration from others? Tell about someone whose example has actually been a means of your drawing similar strength from God for yourself.

Related Readings

Matthew 24:42-44 Hebrews 12:1-6 James 1:12

Prayer to the King

Dear Lord, help us not to neglect to receive a steady inflow of Your power and strength during days of calm, so that we will be able to stand in the day of crisis. Help us to be encouraged by each other, but ultimately to look to Your indwelling Spirit for our strength. Through Christ our Lord, Amen.

Note

1. William Shakespeare, *Julius Caesar*, Act IV, Scene iii.

41

The Time Is Now

SCRIPTURE READING:

And while they were going away to make the purchase, the bridegroom came, and those who were ready went in with him to the wedding feast; and the door was shut. And later the other virgins also came, saying, "Lord, lord, open up for us." But he answered and said, "Truly I say to you, I do not know you." Be on the alert then, for you do not know the day nor the hour.

MATTHEW 25:10-13

The irony of the parable of the bridesmaids is that half of those who actually longed for the coming of the bridegroom were not prepared for him. "The door was shut" are solemn words—both when we apply them to not being ready for judgment day, and to missed opportunities when the Lord breaks into our lives daily, hourly, momentarily—and we are not ready.

Sobering as the story is, I interpret it to be one of Jesus' most positive parables. It is not a negative thing to teach us to "be on the alert." I have a friend who precedes any significant statement she makes with, "Are you ready for this?" The question is a good one. How ready are we for what will happen to us and around us? So often I have heard people say, "I just was not ready for that! I was caught off guard." The lack of preparedness can minimize the truly creative opportunities in life. My friend's question is the very good question that Jesus asks in the parable.

There is no more poignant picture in Scripture than the five foolish maids standing at the door, rapping with importunity, lights now blazing brightly. They can hear the joy of the wedding banquet, the laughter, the music and dancing. But the door is closed.

Tennyson caught the pathos of the closed door:

> Late, late, so late! And dark the night and
> chill!
> Late, late, so late! But we can enter still.
> Too late, too late! Ye cannot enter now.
> No light had we: for this we do repent;
> And learning this, the bridegroom will
> relent.
> Too late, too late! Ye cannot enter now.

No light: So late! And dark and chill the
night!
O let us in that we may find the light!
Too late, too late! Ye cannot enter now.
Have we not heard the bridegroom is so
sweet?
O let us in, tho' late, to kiss his feet!
No, no, too late! Ye cannot enter now.[1]

The closed door in this parable says much more about human nature than about God's graciousness. There is a time when it's too late. Not for God, but for us. The abundant life is offered to us, but we can miss the overtures of God each day. The issue is that repeated resistance results in a life that cannot appropriate the invitation to live forever with God after death. If we constantly say no to Him in our daily lives, it will be impossible to say yes when the midnight hour of our physical demise occurs.

But in another perspective, it's never too late, not as long as we can breathe a breath and listen to the warning of this parable. It sounds an alarm. Here is God's personal word. Are we ready? Why not settle this once and for all! The tragic unpreparedness of the bridesmaids need not be our condition.

The question we must answer is: Are we sharing the joy of the Bridegroom right now? Or are we standing outside, feeling excluded and unacceptable? This need not be our condition. The parable zeros in on us, not at the door seeking entrance, but at the time of our invitation to join the wedding party. It is the hour of preparation right now. Perhaps it's not as late as we thought. We can receive the oil of preparedness in full measure right now. The Holy Spirit is infringing on our consciousness. We can be filled—in fact, remember that Paul commanded us to keep on being "filled with the Spirit" (Eph. 5:18). The result will be a new preparedness for life—now and forever.

Once we have received the limitless power of the Lord within, we will be ready for His approach around us. Right at this moment, the good news is being sounded: "Behold the Bridegroom is coming!" It's an exciting delight to be able to say, "Lord, I'm ready! Ready for anything and anyone! Lead on!"

Kingdom Thinking

1. Has a life experience ever caught you off guard and vulnerable? What would you do to prepare for such an event if you could live that time over again?

2. What implication for the way we live daily is the fact that Jesus said we do not know the day or the hour of His coming?

3. Do you think it's possible for Christians to dwell so much on the anticipated return of Christ or the end of the world that we neglect the daily opportunities He

brings us for earthly ministries and this worldly service to others?

Related Readings

Joel 3:14-17 John 14:1-6 Revelation 20:11-13

Prayer to the King

O Lord, we confess that we are a people of missed opportunities, tardy arrivals, late awareness. We praise You for Your grace in holding open the door; help us not to trade on Your patience by deliberately delaying to enter in. Grant that we may act in the present in order to prepare for our future with You. In Jesus' name, Amen.

Note

1. The novice's song to Guinevere in "The Idylls of the King" by Lord Alfred Tennyson.

42

The Elder Brother in Us

SCRIPTURE READING:

Now his older son was in the field, and when he came and approached the house, he heard music and dancing. And he summoned one of the servants and began inquiring what these things might be. And he said to him. "Your brother has come, and your father has killed the fattened calf, because he has received him back safe and sound." But he became angry, and was not willing to go in; and his father came out and began entreating him.

LUKE 15:25-28

The parable of the elder brother is actually "the rest of the story" of the parable of the prodigal son. We have chosen to include it here in Part III on "Riches in the Lord's Treasury" because it speaks so eloquently of our treasures in the Kingdom. In this chapter, we will focus on the more obvious traits of the elder brother, and in the next, on his deeper underlying problem.

The elder brother was "in the field." Not surprising. He is responsibility and industriousness personified. Life is serious business. He has work to do, duties to accomplish. All the time the younger son was off squandering his portion of the inheritance, the older son was keeping the farm. And for good reason. When the wealth was divided, as the firstborn, he received a double portion—two-thirds of the property. Deuteronomy 21:17 made that very clear. The elder son was not working those fields out of love and faithfulness to his father. They belonged to him! That's why he was working so hard. But like his younger brother, he forgot that what he had was a trust from the father to be enjoyed with thankfulness.

The elder brother is indignant when the servant tells him the reason for the celebration. His brother was back! Why should he not be indignant when he returned from his hard work to find a party in full swing for the brother who had forsaken his work? Indignation became rage. That squanderer, loose-liver, irresponsible spender deserved no party. The elder brother would have no part of that. He would not dignify the celebration with his presence. He turned on his heel in consternation, white-hot anger flowing through his veins.

And there's the father pursuing him as he had run toward the other lost son, entreating him, "Come to the party!" The father took it for granted that his older son would be ecstatic over his brother's safe return. If not that, surely he would share the joy of his father's heart.

Not so. Every word in Luke 15:29 and 30 exposes his self-justifying relationship to the father. In his indignant wrath, he includes accusations of sins we have not been told the prodigal son committed. Harlots? Riotous living? Were these the elder brother's own sins of fantasy he read into the record of what his brother had done? Projection. His vitriolic tirade tells us more about him than about his brother.

The elder brother is self-righteous. His status with the father, he thought, was dependent on his service and obedience. Completely missing his father's gracious heart, he was determined to be impeccable and flawless—all so that he could maintain his status on the basis of his own adequacy.

He was proud. If our goodness is our status, what's left but to extol and worship our accomplishment? We soon build our whole life around arrogant self-satisfaction. At his core, the elder brother was no different from the lost son prior to his return to the father.

His pride led to bitter judgmentalism. The lost and broken are the way they are because they are profligate, and because they didn't work as hard as we have. It's their own fault.

Empathy and identification flow together as we watch the elder brother. Is the elder brother a look in the mirror for us? Are we forced to see more than we want to acknowledge? Are we upset when someone "undeserving" is elevated as a model of coming home to the Father? Do we somehow resent having "stayed home" and missed out on the life of a prodigal? Are the lines of pride, judgmentalism and self-sufficiency cut, like the plowman's furrows, in our brow?

To ask such questions is to risk looking at a side of us we would rather not face. The primary safeguard against seeing the traits of the elder brother lurking deep within our hearts is to experience to the fullest the grace of the Father. Only grace can enable and ennoble us to accept other prodigals with the love the Father has shown to us.

Kingdom Thinking

1. What riches did the elder brother have, and what made him unable to appreciate them?

2. Note the beginning of the chapter in which this parable is set (Luke 15:1,2). In context, who do you think the younger and the elder brothers represent?

3. Meditate on each trait described in this chapter—anger, self-justification, pride, judgmentalism. Ask God to rid your heart of any "elder brother" tendencies you may see in yourself.

Related Readings

Acts 13:44-48   Romans 2:28—3:2   James 3:13-18

Prayer to the King

We do not pray to be prodigals, O Lord, but we pray that we will not envy them Your love and acceptance. Help us to confess our own prodigal thoughts, and to rejoice in the common salvation available both to those who have stayed home, and to those who return. In Jesus' name, Amen.

43

What About Me?

SCRIPTURE READING:

And he said to him, "My child, you have always been with me, and all that is mine is yours. But we had to be merry and rejoice, for this brother of yours was dead and has begun to live, and was lost and has been found."

LUKE 15:31,32

The face of the elder brother is a revealing study as he storms around outside the party in honor of the prodigal son who has come home. The lines of pride, judgmentalism and self-sufficiency are clearly evident in his unhappy face. His jaw is set with serious determination. Most frightening of all, he has no joy in his eyes.

How could it be that a celebration would be given for a son who was so profligate? Has the world gone mad?

Are there no standards? Has his father lost all his senses in sentimentality? What the elder brother was really saying was, "What about me, Father? Don't you admire my faithfulness? Have I worked all these years for nothing? You've never given me an appreciation banquet!"

Underneath the unenviable behavior of the elder brother, a raw nerve has been exposed. It is a deeply rooted insecurity. He has an insatiable need for his father's approval and esteem.

The pain in the father's voice expresses his dawning realization that his elder son did not share his heart of love. Feel the heartbreak of the father, more excruciating than when the younger son left home. He realized that his elder son had never *been* at home—really. Competition and rivalry with his younger brother had been brewing for a long time. The old insecurity and fears of childhood had returned in full force. Did the father love the younger son more than him?

At the beginning of this book, we described the extravagant, prodigious love of the father as the primary "prodigal" element of the story. Now he turns the full force of this compassion toward his elder son. "My child," he calls him. The Greek word is *teknon*, a term of tender endearment. He explains how he has loved him all along. All things were his.

The elder son's work had not been out of gratitude. He had not accepted the father's daily flow of provision, sustenance and opportunity as evidence of love.

Most of all, he did not share the father's love for his brother. Note the disturbing difference between the elder son's "your son" and the father's "your brother."

We must admit that we ask questions similar to those the elder brother must have asked. Is there no retribution for what people do with the inheritance of life? If a rascal such as the younger brother can slip back into an equal status with us, why work and do what's right? Deathbed conversions make us wonder about our lifelong efforts to serve God and to live a productive life.

Aren't there some rewards for years of faithfulness? Yes, the joy of fellowship with our Father through the years. But when our own self-generated piety, morality and religion keep us from grace, we might as well have been squandering in the far country. We elder brothers leave the father without ever leaving the farm. The distance is measured by our efforts to be adequate on our own, constantly calculated by comparison with others.

"A darkened heart," says Augustine, "is the far country, for it is not by our feet but by our affections that we either leave Thee or return unto Thee."

One of the most poignant ways of feeling the full impact of what Jesus is saying about elder-brother tendencies in us is to imagine what might have happened if the returning son had met his older brother on the way, before receiving the loving embrace of the father. The younger son never would have made it home. Living as a starving pig in a pigsty would be better than being starved for love and being accepted by his brother.

It sets our imagination racing. How many needy people never make it back to the Father's heart because of us elder brothers in the church, the family or society?

Considering these implications should be enough to bring us to the party! If we want fellowship with our heavenly Father, that's where we have to go—to the party, leaving our fussy indignation behind. There is good news for the elder brother in each of us: The Father loves us all equally. We need not work for His approval; it is there all along.

Kingdom Thinking

1. What spiritual riches at the hand of your heavenly Father do you appreciate most?
2. In light of Luke 7:36-50, would you expect the younger or the elder brother to love their father more?
3. What is the antidote for always needing to be reassured of God's love and constantly feeling insecure in our relationship to Him?

Related Readings

Matthew 9:9-13 Matthew 18:21,22 Galatians 4:1-7

Prayer to the King

Grant us, Holy Father, such a deep and abiding gratitude for our place in Your kingdom that we react only with joy when others are also established in Your grace. All we like sheep have gone astray; help all likewise to welcome each other back into the fold. In the name of the Great Shepherd of our souls, Amen.

44

The Joy of Ambition

SCRIPTURE READING:

For it is just like a man about to go on a journey, who called his own slaves, and entrusted his possessions to them. And to one he gave five talents, to another, two, and to another, one, each according to his own ability; and he went on his journey. Immediately the one who had received the five talents went and traded with them, and gained five more talents. In the same manner the one who had received the two talents gained two more....[And the] master said to him, "Well done, good and faithful slave; you were faithful with a few things, I will put you in charge of many things; enter into the joy of your master."

MATTHEW 25:14-17,21

The man across the lunch table didn't need to tell me he was despondent. It was written on his face and expressed in his body language. "I used to be a joyous Christian," he explained. But now his life seemed flat and dull. "I wish you could help me find the joy I used to have," he said.

I conclude from the parable of the talents that people such as this despondent man have a lack of ambition! The word "ambition" has become tainted in our time. Ambition has been made antithetical to authentic spirituality. The real issue, however, is the *focus* of our ambition. If it is for Christ and His cause, ambition is baptized with His affirmation and power.

The word "ambition" comes from the Latin word *ambitio*—to go around. It means eager movement around the opportunities of life in order to achieve a desired goal. Very often, joyless Christians have not been ambitious for Christ in the way a person goes about seeking worldly achievements. The man whose Christianity had gone flat had not been "moving around" with his faith. He had not ambitiously sought to share his joy, or to take risks to be spiritually productive. He had not involved himself in the lives of hurting people, and had never felt the satisfaction of being a reconciler of broken relationships.

A "talent" was a monetary unit in Jesus' day, worth perhaps one thousand dollars in today's money. The five-talent and the two-talent men in Jesus' parable were ambitious for their master. The first two servants moved about eagerly to earn a good investment, and they doubled the funds that had been entrusted to them, earning the approval of the master and greater responsibility as well.

Our natural endowments, plus the gift of the indwelling Spirit, make us the spiritually wealthy of the world. I suggest that the talents in Jesus' parable represent the gift of the abundant life He entrusts to us. Having the ambition to live it to the fullest and to share it with others is the qualification of "entering the joy of the Master" (see Matt. 25:21). On the other hand, many Christians have buried their talents in beautifully carved boxes as though to conserve their faith. They forget that they exist to multiply the talent of the abundant life in the world. So they miss out on the joy of adventurous living.

Do you think of Christianity as an adventure for ambitious people? For many Christians, it is a set of creeds, rules and regulations, the institutional church and dreary obligations. We think of our faith as part of maintaining the sanity of the status quo. If we can just get through our lives without too many crises or stretching challenges, we will be satisfied. We want to do reasonably well at our profession, raise a decent family, keep out of trouble and retire comfortably. We take few risks for Christ, and we have little concept of the joy of the abundant—and the ambitious—life.

God can guide a moving person. He can take a person such as Paul, who expressed his ambitious nature in the wrong way, and change his direction so he can say, "How my ambitions have changed! All I want now is to live the adventure of the abundant life!"

If ambition has enabled you to be a success, then surrender the opportunities your realm of responsibility gives you. The Lord knows that human positions of power and influence can be used for His glory if we will entrust them to Him. In every company, community or structure of society, people are in strategic positions who have an opportunity to affect the lives of millions. The church and society can be dramatically changed—and we can experience the joy of the abundant life—if we thank God for the ambition He has entrusted to us and use it to spread that life.

Each of us has an irreplaceable calling in God's plan. Two things are required: to ask God what He wants us to do, and to "move about," doing it with joy!

Kingdom Thinking

1. Does the word "ambition" have a positive or a negative connotation for you?

2. Can you give an example of a person who has been ambitious and successful both in this world and in spiritual matters?

3. Are there spheres of Christian service to which

you aspire that would require gifts you haven't yet developed? What are some practical steps toward reaching such "ambitions"? (Consider 1 Corinthians 12:1-10 and Romans 12.)

Related Reading

Galatians 6:6-10 Colossians 3:12-17 Titus 2:11-14

Prayer to the King

Give us zeal for Your kingdom, O God! Grant that we may take the energy and enthusiasm so many have for this world's goods and channel them into ambitious plans and projects and works in behalf of others. Help us not to lose heart in doing good, knowing that in due season we shall reap if we do not grow weary. Through Jesus we pray, Amen.

45

We Are Accountable!

SCRIPTURE READING:

But he who received the one talent went away and dug in the ground, and hid his master's money....and said, "Master, I knew you to be a hard man, reaping where you did not sow, and gathering where you scattered no seed. And I was afraid, and went away and hid your talent in the ground; see, you have what is yours." But his master answered..."Cast out the worthless slave into the outer darkness."

MATTHEW 25:18,24,25,26,30

When we understand Jesus' use of the concept of "talents" as our abundant relationship with Him and the authority to communicate His love to others, then we are all talented. The five- and the two-talent men of the parable are used only to set the stage for the one-talent man's refusal to use and invest his talent.

The one-talent man hangs back with customary reticence. He is not eager, as are the other two. Smarting under the affirmation given them, he is quickly formulating his defensive explanation of what he had not done with his one talent. We are astonished at his ready projection when he is called to report: "I knew you to be a hard man" (Matt. 25:24). Actually, just the opposite was true. The master had sown generously with his investment in all three servants, and had graciously left them in charge of sorting the chaff from the wheat of alternative possibilities of developing his investment. But the third servant projects his fear and presses an image on the master to protect his own frightened self-image. And the master deals out punishment according to the servant's idea of what he was like.

The point of the parable is for those of us who may not consider ourselves especially endowed with human capacities. Too many of us allow what we think we cannot do to dissuade us from doing what we can. We do little or nothing because others seem so much more gifted. Because we cannot be spectacular, we refuse to be significant in our assigned realm. Soon we blame others, conditions or our circumstances. Eventually, we blame God.

The truth is that if we have met the Savior and allowed Him to live His life through us, we have been talented beyond calculation. And this parable clearly teaches that we are accountable for the way we use the talent of the abundant life. Christ poured out the power of the Holy Spirit (see Acts 2:33) not only to enable the ministry of the infant Early Church, but also to assure a return on the investment of the Church's stewardship of the new life. We are accountable every day, and on the ultimate day when we leave this earthly phase of eternal life to go on to the next. The daily and final question when we die physically is: What have we done with the talent entrusted to us?

As was the case with the talent-burying servant, excuses and projected blame will not do. God has sown the gospel in us. He has winnowed the chaff from the grain through life's challenges to give us human illustrations from our own experience, so that we might share what Christ can mean for others. He does expect reproduction! We will have no lasting joy if we bury our talent in the ground of refusal.

Recently, our congregation became aware that eighty-five percent of the people in the Hollywood area have no church home and do not attend regularly. This motivated us to start a program called "Operation Come and See." It is based on John 1:45,46. Philip shared his excitement about Christ with Nathanael, and asked him to go with him to hear the Master. Nathanael's response was, "Can any good thing come out of Nazareth?" Winsome Philip's simple answer was "Come and see."

We asked our church people to identify seven people out of the staggering percentage to come to church with them: to "come and see" and to hear about the abundant life. The most gratifying thing to me was how many church members dug up their talent and used it. In many cases, it had been dormant in the ground of respectable churchmanship for years. Relationships with friends, neighbors and fellow workers were established on a deeper level. Conversations about what faith in Christ means flowed naturally before and after the contemporary Nathanaels were brought to church.

What the master said to the reproductive servants, the Lord wants to say to us: "Well done. Excellent! You are a devoted, full-of-faith, persistent and venturesome steward of the life I lived and died to provide. In sharing what you have, you have allowed My joy-beat to be the pulse of your heart. You have been faithful in this; now I will give you greater opportunities."

Kingdom Thinking

1. Have you ever been involved in introducing someone to Jesus, or in providing a listening ear to someone who is hurting? Although none of us wants to

boast as though such an experience is a "notch on our gun," share with others how this made you feel.

2. We often "undersell" what we have as Christians and what we might be able to share with others. List several special joys you have because you are a Christian, and discuss how you might share them with others.

Related Readings

2 Kings 7:1-9 Luke 6:36 2 Timothy 2:19-21

Prayer to the King

Deliver us, O Lord, from the tendency to deny our gifts. Help us to so experience the joy of the abundant life that our hearts overflow with the passion to share it with others. Give us sensitivity to the needs of those about us, and the willingness to invest ourselves in them for Your sake.
In Jesus' name we pray, Amen.

Part IV

Growing in the Lord's Vineyard

46

Hard Hearts, Shallow Souls

Scripture Reading:

Behold, the sower went out to sow; and as he sowed, some seeds fell beside the road, and the birds came and ate them up. And others fell upon the rocky places, where they did not have much soil; and immediately they sprang up, because they had no depth of soil. But when the sun had risen, they were scorched; and because they had no root, they withered away. And others fell among the thorns, and the thorns came up and choked them out.

Matthew 13:3-7

The Lord was enjoying unprecedented popularity. People came from near and far. The crowds forced Him to utilize a small fishing boat as His pulpit. A few feet from shore, He was able to scrutinize the throng. How serious were they? Did they really know what He was saying? A life-situation parable was being dramatized nearby on the hillside. A sower was sowing seed on different kinds of ground. The scene gave Jesus the perfect vehicle to expose four different kinds of spiritual soil—the hearts of His hearers.

Four very different ways of hearing the God who speaks are described here. We need not try to fit ourselves into only one of the categories. A bit of all four resides in each of us. Our heart, in the Hebrew understanding, is the seat of intellect, emotion and will. What Jesus has to say to us must thunder through to all aspects of our hearts if we are to be made whole.

The seeds that fall on the trodden path dance on the surface, gusted to and fro by the winds. The birds flutter above and then descend to pluck up a ready meal. The seed and the soil need each other, but there is no productive contact. The marble-hard surface resists implantation (see Matt. 13:19).

Life can do just that to our hearts. Each failure or rejection impacts a crust of resistance to vulnerability. We develop defenses to cope. The pity of it is that we lose selectivity. The good and the bad are held off with equal firmness. Such Christians are similar to Jesus' friends and neighbors in His hometown of Nazareth. "He did not many mighty works there because of their unbelief" (Matt. 13:58, *KJV*).

The second category of hearers in Jesus' parable is the shallow heart. Seeds scattered on soil over bedrock found enough soil to take root, but because the roots are not allowed to grow deeply and are denied the replenishment of depth nourishment, the surface plant withers in the sun. It cannot sustain its initial growth; it is "only temporary" (v. 21).

Remember that the heart is the inner core of intellect, emotion and will. If any one aspect of the heart is shallow and undeveloped, the seed of the Word may experience immediate growth but no lasting maturity. Take the emotional Christian. His encounter with Christ has been warm and exciting, but it won't last until he has an intellectual and volitional conversion. The same is true of the intellectual Christian who has never allowed Christ to deal with his feelings. Some of us have been on an intellectual head trip so long we cannot respond to life with an authentic expression of our feelings. And volitional rock is equally dangerous. We can be intellectually sound and emotionally freed, but become withered Christians if we refuse to do God's will in the painful areas of obedience.

On the other hand, it's possible for this volitional soil to provide a temporary seedbed while our minds and emotions form the rock beneath. We are living in a day of unprecedented activism and social responsibility. Some need to hear what Napoleon once said of himself: "Great men are meteors that consume themselves to light the earth. This is my burned out hour." Burned-out Christians are activists whose roots are not firmly planted in intellectual and emotional maturity.

Finally, the fourth category is the thorny soil. Some seed fell on ground that was already infested by weed seeds. Both the good and the bad seed would come up, but eventually the nutrients and resources of the soil would be sapped by the thorns. Likewise, many voices are clamoring for our attention, competing with the seed of the Word. We can become so overinvolved that we cannot hear what our Lord is saying to us. The circuits get overloaded, and eventually jam. Anxiety, riches (see v. 22), pleasure-seeking—such distractions can become thorns that must be weeded out in order to provide nourishment for the seed of the Word.

Fortunately, there is a better way. God's Word need not fall on hard or shallow or weed-choked ground. That kind of good soil is the subject of our next chapter.

Kingdom Thinking

1. Think of an example—perhaps from your own life—that illustrates:
   a. A heart that resists the Word.
   b. A heart that at first receives the Word, but the experience doesn't last.
   c. A heart that's too busy or otherwise distracted.
2. If the condition of the heart is so important in

how a person receives the Word, how can we cultivate receptive hearts in those about us with whom we would like to share the blessings of the Kingdom?

Related Readings

Exodus 7:8-13 Mark 6:45-52 Hebrews 3:12-19

Prayer to the King

Life is filled with stress and pressure, O Lord. We need Your help in keeping our hearts receptive to Your Word amid the other words that clamor for our attention. Grant us Your grace to keep our hearts tender, Your Spirit to provide deep, newly plowed soil, and Your implanted Word to produce roots in our lives. Through Jesus we pray, Amen.

47

The Good Earth

SCRIPTURE READING:

Behold, the sower went out to sow; And others [some seed] fell on the good soil, and yielded a crop, some a hundredfold, some sixty, and some thirty. He who has ears, let him hear.

MATTHEW 13:3,8,9

The television interviewer asked me to prepare several questions I would be willing to answer on a talk show. They were to be questions that would explore aspects of my life as a speaker and writer. One of the questions I submitted caused no small alarm among the people preparing the script, for I suggested they ask, "What has God been saying to you these days?"

"What do you mean?" I was asked. "Does God really talk to you? When do you hear Him? How do you know it's His voice?" I did my best to clarify. No audible voice—a whisper in my soul, fresh thought, insight and wisdom, convictions from ancient truth. And more than that, a communication from God that comes as I read Scripture, take time for meditative prayer, listen to people, observe the Almighty's signature in nature and live in depth in life's challenges.

All this comes to those whose hearts are like the fourth kind of ground Jesus described in the parable of the soils. The good soil is the listening heart. When the Lord asked Solomon to name the one blessing he needed most, the young king responded, "Give Thy servant an understanding heart to judge Thy people" (1 Kings 3:9). The Hebrew means a listening or hearing heart. Jesus wanted this for everyone who thronged along the seashore when He gave them the parable of the soils.

Mark's version of this parable stresses receptivity as the basic ingredient of the good soil (see Mark 4:1-12). Luke quotes Jesus' illuminating comment that "the seed in the good soil, these are the ones who have heard the word in an honest and good heart, and hold it fast, and bear fruit with perseverance" (Luke 8:15). Considered together, the three versions stress that a hearing heart receives, responds, reproduces and is relentless in its drive to take root and to produce fruit.

A hearing heart responds to the Word with sincerity. It is an honest and good heart. Not double minded or seeking to serve two masters. It is a prayerful heart, holding fast what God has said, pondering it until it yields the gift of understanding.

Action is the final step of hearing. God speaks to those involved in bearing fruit in themselves and others. The fruit of listening to God is the transformation of character. The more we listen to Him through the Holy Spirit, the more He will work on our personalities. He wants to make us like Jesus. The fruit of the Spirit, the productive result of communication with God, according to Paul, is "love, joy, peace, patience, kindness, goodness, faithfulness, gentleness, self-control" (Gal. 5:22,23). Take this list into dialogue with God in prayer. Ask Him to show you what's lacking and needs growth. Allow Him to give your imagination the picture of what you would be like as a fruit-filled person. Then thank Him that it shall be so!

When we listen to God, He identifies the people He has made ready. He gives us the strategy, words, attitude and love for a liberating friendship with these people. The One who knows the depths of each personality can give us the key to unlock the people He appoints for us to introduce to Him. He "walks us through" our relationships, sensitizing us to the way to communicate profoundly. The people who listen to God are able to listen to people. When we speak and share, we will be on target. People will be changed.

God is speaking to each of us right now as we read

this. What does He have to say? He wants us to know how much He loves us. For our sins, He wants to give us calvary's assurance. His perspective and power are offered for our possibilities and problems. He wants to reign supreme in our hearts so we can pray, "Your Kingdom come, Your will be done." The Lord is ready to guide the future. He offers insight, discernment and wisdom for the alternatives that face us. Most of all, He wants to give us Himself.

God has spent a long time plowing, blasting the bedrock, weeding out the thorns of the soil of our hearts. He has made us good soil. Now He has something to say. Are we listening? If so, God will whisper in your delights, speak in your problems and shout in your perplexities!

Kingdom Thinking

1. Do you find it strange, awkward or mystical to think in terms of God's speaking to us? Can you put into your own words what this might mean? Do you experience it in your own everyday life? If so, how and under what conditions?

2. Describe what it's like when you want very much to make yourself heard, but the person you're speaking to isn't really listening. Do you think God experiences similar frustration with us?

3. What conditions of the heart can make it diffi-

cult to really hear what other people are saying? How can we increase our ability to be good listeners?

Related Readings

Matthew 7:24-27 Matthew 13:10-15 Mark 4:33,34

Prayer to the King

We praise You, God of the good soil, for all that has been done to prepare our hearts to hear You. Thank You for childhood direction, the displays of Your grace in others, the signs of Your creative power in nature. Grant that we may respond to these influences with hearts that hear and wills that bear fruit. Through Christ our Lord, Amen.

48

The Harbinger of Hope

SCRIPTURE READING:

And He was saying, "The kingdom of God is like a man who casts seed upon the soil; and goes to bed at night and gets up by day, and the seed sprouts up and grows—how, he himself does not know."

MARK 4:26,27

If I could have the confidence in the midst of crises and challenges that I have after they are over, how much more abundant my life would be. I am much better at retrospective interpretation of what God has done than I am at relaxed insight about what He's doing. I share this because I suspect that many who read this can identify with me. If so, Jesus' parable of the seed growing secretly is the Great Physician's personal prescription, His harbinger of hope.

The parable follows naturally our previous reflections on the sower and the soil. The focus is still on planting the seed of the Word of God—the seed of the Kingdom, or the reign, rule and triumph of God in us, between us and in society. Only Mark records this parable. Did he see the principle of the seed growing secretly as having worked in his own life? I think so. After having had the seed of the Kingdom planted during the exciting days of the infant Church, Mark had gone through a time of disappointment and failure. He defected from the mission with Paul. But, with the help of Barnabas, and then Peter, he had made a new start. Now, I can imagine that he smiled and felt a surge of delight as he wrote down Jesus' parable. It was his story. It had happened to him!

And the story is the dramatic narrative of the Incarnation. Jesus Himself planted the seed of Himself in the soil of history, over hill and dale in every heart that would listen. He planted Himself on a bare hill called calvary. The world has never been the same: a band of disciples, a Spirit-filled church at Pentecost, a missionary movement to the reaches of the world, and now the only hope for our sick and suffering society. Two thousand years, but a moment in eternity beyond calculated time.

Why does it take so long? We are chained to our conception of progress, bound by our lack of vision. God is working out His purposes. The seed is planted, the blade is piercing the hard crust of human resistance. The world cannot stamp it out. It is growing. The kingdoms of this world are becoming the kingdom of our Lord!

In this context, we can enjoy the persistence of God in us. When was the seed planted in you? It happened to me as a freshman in college. I heard the good news of God's love in Christ and had my imagination turpentined by a fellowship of Christians who gave me a picture of what God meant my life to be. I accepted Christ as my Savior. Trusting Him as Lord of my life has not come easily. Each new surrender of the facets and relationships of my life fertilizes the seed.

Now, we are ready to see what the parable of spontaneous growth has to say about our impatience with life and the future. The parable of the growth of the seed teaches us that what God guides, He provides. Between the planting and the harvesting is a waiting period when He is at work, and we must wait. Peace is God's gift for the interface between the launching of what He wills and its fulfillment in His way and in His time.

The process by which the seed is planted, grows and is harvested tells us that God knows what He is doing. There is order in the created world. Our lives are not determined by a nameless fate. There are physical and spiritual laws that govern the levels of plant, animal and human life. At every moment of our anxious uncertainty, God is arranging, motivating, inspiring, preparing.

Rollo May, a psychologist, suggested that our ability to hope and our susceptibility to anxiety are two sides of the same capacity. Our power of expectation engendered by the Spirit must be equalled with the assurance that what we have been led to expect will evolve at the right time and way. If we didn't have the daring to believe that things can be changed, we'd never be anxious. But the restless bedfellow of anxiety is worry, and worry is sin; it is the outward expression of inner anxiety. Do we have confidence in God? In the Word as the seed of the Kingdom? What more must God do to prove Himself? More than Creation, the Incarnation, calvary, the Resurrection, the gift of the Holy Spirit?

The parable of the growth of the seed is the basis of future hope, rather than "future shock." It is an antidote to anxiety, an invitation to trust and the permission to dream!

Kingdom Thinking

1. How are anxiety and hope related? How can we distinguish between them?
2. Reflecting on troubled times in your own life, are

you able to see how God brought you through them? Are there even some blessings that came out of them?

3. Have you ever known of worry to cause physical debilitation?

4. Why is worry a sin?

Related Readings

Psalm 23 Jeremiah 29:7-11 Matthew 6:25-34

Prayer to the King

Dear Father, Your care of Your people was evidenced long before our own concerns arose. For ages, You have parted waters and opened graves and inspired faith. Help us to accept this saving history as a source of confidence and abiding trust. In His trustworthy name we pray, Amen.

49

The Eclipse of Anxiety

SCRIPTURE READING:

The kingdom of God is like a man who casts seed upon the soil; and....The soil produces crops by itself; first the blade, then the head, then the mature grain in the head. But when the crop permits, he immediately puts in the sickle, because the harvest has come.

MARK 4:26-29

Once, during an anxious period of waiting, a friend said a harsh thing to me that finally gave me comfort: "If God wants it, no one can stop it. If He doesn't, there's no way you could pull it off anyway. So relax!" The parable of the seed growing secretly contains some very specific steps for relaxing and living with the tension of unfulfilled hopes.

First, evaluate the seed, considering it carefully. Is what we want an extension of the Kingdom as best we can understand? Does it fit with God's purposes? Will it bring us and others closer to Him? Is He guiding you?

Second, once we are sure of the seed, plant it courageously. Commit it unreservedly to God. Do all you can, then leave the results to Him. We cannot hold on to the seed in our feverish, sweaty hands and expect the earth to do anything. Put the seed into the resourceful soil of the power of God.

Third, allow the seed to die as a part of the germination. Jesus said, "Unless a grain of wheat falls into the earth and dies, it remains by itself alone; but if it dies, it bears much fruit" (John 12:24). He followed this counsel immediately with the challenging statement, "He who hates his life in this world shall keep it to life eternal" (v. 25). "Hate" here means to love less—to love God and His plan for us more than we love our own lives. We cannot clutch the seed in our clenched fist and thrust it into the ground, expecting it to grow when our hand of impervious determination keeps God's own soil from touching it.

Fourth, leave the committed seed and its new roots in the ground! Our temptation is to pull up the plant to see if it is growing. It may be fascinating to look at the vivid, light green life pressing out from the seed or bulb, but keeping it out of the soil is a sure way to kill future growth. The farmer in the parable went about his regular duties while the seed grew. He didn't dig up the seed each day to see if there had been any progress.

Fifth, cultivate the ground. When the first evidence of the blade appears above the surface of the soil, rejoice, but know that God intends to grow a fully mature plant. Don't harvest the blade. The fruit of faithfulness is in the grain. Watch the blade grow with adoration and praise. It is a portent of fulfillment.

Last, enjoy the harvest. Often we are so worried about the next challenge that we can't enjoy what God has done with previously committed concerns. I am alarmed at how little I remember of how God has worked in the past when I face difficulties in which I need confidence that He is at work right now. How could I forget?

But I do forget, even though I have experienced the truth of this parable repeatedly in my own life. Several years ago my wife was seriously ill with cancer. Her own prayers about the future gave her a firm confidence that she would be well. She placed the seed of that God-given vision in the ground. Together, we thanked God that what He told us would come true. The long period of surgeries, treatments and therapy seemed endless. The temptation to fear was ever present. But God was faithful to His promise. His timing was not ours; but now she is well again, healed by the Great Physician through the power of the Holy Spirit.

As a spiritual leader, as a parent, I have to remind myself repeatedly of the faithful working of the seed I entrust to God. I try to remember Paul's strong statement, "I am sure that he who began a good work in you will bring it to completion" (Phil. 1:6, *RSV*). God is not finished either with me or with those I love. The challenge is to trust that He always finishes what He starts. The future is in His hands!

Do you believe that God can cause the earth to produce crops "by itself" (Mark 4:28)? Then why do you still have a seed in your hand? Thrust it into the ground! You can live without anxiety.

Kingdom Thinking

1. What kinds of trials or tests make you most vulnerable to anxiety?

2. Single out a specific concern in your life. Using the help of others, determine the difference between giving way to anxiety on the one hand and being indifferent on the other.

3. Pray with other Christians about specific concerns, paying special attention to the need to let the "seed" grow as God wills, and releasing all your anxiety and need to control the outcome.

Related Readings

Philippians 1:12-20 Philippians 4:4-7 Hebrews 13:5,6

Prayer to the King

Help me, O Lord, to pray honestly this prayer of relinquishment: I pray for my loved ones, but I release them to You. I pray for daily bread, but I will not be anxious about it. I ask for peace on earth, good will toward men, but I release myself from having to bear the earth and others on my shoulders. I am ready to be used, for I trust the strong name of Jesus, in whose name I pray, Amen.

50

Dangerous Christians

SCRIPTURE READING:

The kingdom of heaven may be compared to a man who sowed good seed in his field. But while men were sleeping, his enemy came and sowed tares also among the wheat, and went away. And the slaves of the landowner came and said to him, "Sir, did you not sow good seed in your field? How then does it have tares?" But he said,... "Allow both to grow together until the harvest."

MATTHEW 13:24,25,27,29,30

Some time ago, I had the questionable notoriety of being listed as one of the ten most dangerous leaders of the Church in America. My vision for the renewal of the Church ran counter to the ideas of the author of the list. I gained some comfort in the fact that my friend Billy Graham was also listed, along with eight others whom I love and admire. The list maker's purge of the leadership of the Church was not taken seriously, and soon was publicly repudiated as one more of his vitriolic pronouncements.

Who are the really dangerous people in the Church? Or, to put it more personally: Who are the dangerous people in your congregation and mine? In the parable of the wheat and the tares, they are identified as tares or weeds. The greatest threat to any farmer in Jesus' day was that an enemy might express his hostility, anger or retribution by sowing weeds in his field of wheat. Jesus wanted His followers to ask themselves, "Am I a wheat or a weed in the Lord's field? Am I an authentic follower of the Lord or the planting of the devil?"

Every congregation has a group of these tares, or dangerous people, and a group that can be called good wheat. It makes all the difference for now and eternity which group we're in. The great challenge is to liberate people from the category of the tares to the category of the wheat.

The Church of Jesus Christ is made up of inside-outsiders and inside-insiders. The first group makes up the most dangerous people in the Church. They are the tares. Only two people have the prerogative of determining which group you're in—Jesus Christ and you.

The inside-outsider and the inside-insider often look alike, sound similar and both believe in Jesus Christ. Their relationship to Him as Lord, however, couldn't be more dissimilar. What is the difference?

The inside-outsider is in the Church but outside a deep, intimate relationship with Christ. He believes that Jesus Christ is the Savior of the world, but has never come to know Him as the Lord of his life. There never has been a time of complete commitment of all he or she has and is. The power of the Christian life is experienced in daily, specific surrender of the needs, challenges, problems and opportunities of life. The inside-outsider is inside the Church, but outside of an intimate, impelling, indwelling experience of Christ as Lord.

One of the most gratifying and puzzling phenomena of our time is the great number of church members who are discovering the joy and freedom of committing their lives to Christ. They are discovering the excitement of trusting Christ with their frustrations and fears. Recently, a church member realized the power of Christ and shared the delight of his experience with fellow members at a party. It was very disturbing to some when he said, "I've been a Presbyterian for years. Last week I found out what it's all about to be a Christian. I've always believed that Christ was Savior, but for the first time I *know* He's *my* Savior! It's alarming to think of all the joy I've missed by being an uncommitted church member. Now I know Christ as the Lord of all my relationships and responsibilities."

This church member had become an inside-insider: inside the Church and inside a personal relationship with Christ. He was no longer running his own life. Christ had taken charge as Lord. Before, he had been one of the most dangerous men in the congregation. Why? Because his pretentious facsimile looked like the real thing. And he kept his church locked on dead center. He would not allow it to move beyond what he had experienced.

The Church faces no more crucial issue today than how to make inside-insiders out of inside-outsiders. It's never easy. Inside-outsiders think they have experienced all there is to be discovered in the Christian life. They are dangerous because they want to do God's work in their own strength. It won't work!

Kingdom Thinking

1. On the basis of what's been said in this chapter, define the difference between an "inside-outsider" and an "inside-insider." Do you agree that the "inside-outsider" is a "dangerous" Christian? Why or why not?

2. Can you identify a time when you realized that there was a deeper personal dimension to your relationship with Jesus Christ?

3. Why is it important to realize that only the per-

son and Christ can really determine which category we are in?

Related Readings

Isaiah 55:6-11 Jeremiah 29:11-13 Matthew 13:53-58

Prayer to the King

Dear Father in heaven, it is sometimes easier for me to believe that You forgive the sins of the world than it is to affirm that You gave Your Son for me, personally. Help me to remember that You know the number of the hairs of my head, and that You have my personal well-being at heart. May I respond to this love with heartfelt obedience, rejoicing in the intimate relationship You long to have with Your daughters and sons. Through Christ I pray, Amen.

51

Scandalous Christians

SCRIPTURE READING:

Just as the tares are gathered up and burned with fire, so shall it be at the end of the age. The Son of Man will send forth His angels, and they will gather out of His kingdom all stumbling blocks, and those who commit lawlessness, and will cast them into the furnace of fire;...Then the righteous will shine forth as the sun in the kingdom of their Father. He who has ears, let him hear.

MATTHEW 13:40-43

The disciples could hardly wait to be alone with Jesus to ask for His explanation of the parable of the tares (see Matt. 13:36-43). What He told them was far more than they had anticipated. The question the disciples focused on was, "Are you of the tares or the wheat?" It's no less our question as well.

Jesus went on to identify the tares as "stumbling blocks." The Greek word is *skandalon*. It means a stone of tripping, or a snare—anything that causes a person to stumble. Jesus used the idea in two ways. He knew He was a stumbling block to people who were self-righteous. They "took offense" at Him. He also warned people about being stumbling blocks for others. Both of these are emphasized by the apostle Paul. When Paul reflected on the Incarnation and his people's rejection of the Messiah, he said, "They stumbled over the stumbling stone" (Rom. 9:32). Paul also cautioned about people who obstruct others with stumbling stones—those who "put an obstacle or a stumbling block in a brother's way" (14:13).

Applying all this to the parable of the tares, we must understand that when we refuse to depend personally on the Lord and to enter into an intimate relationship with Him, we become stumbling blocks to others. We become not only dangerous Christians, but also "scandalous" or stumbling-block Christians. It's possible to hear the good news of God's love in Christ without letting Him love us personally in the depth of our need.

It seems ridiculous, but thousands of people attend church and call themselves Christians but never know the joy of abiding in Christ and allowing Him to abide in them. They look and act like wheat, but are tares. Our Lord says to them what He said to Simon Peter when he resisted the necessity of the Cross: "Get behind Me, Satan! You are a stumbling block to Me" (Matt. 16:23). We can be agents of Satan's resistance rather than agents of reconciliation. Until we trip in our efforts to control our own lives and to justify ourselves, we will cause others to stumble over our distorted example.

I meet Christians everywhere who resist the confession of their total dependence on Christ. It's possible to say we believe in Christ when we join the church and then live in our own strength and our own efforts to be adequate by our own talent and moral rectitude. We can have constant relapses into old patterns of self-sufficiency conditioned by training and the values of self-reliance admired in our society. It trips our self-image to accept that there's no way to God except by way of calvary, that we could not think a thought or breathe a breath without God's blessing, and that we cannot accomplish our reason for being without God's transformation of our personality.

Tares become stumbling blocks to others who might otherwise yield to Christ the vital nerve center of their own lives. This explains the checkered pages of Christian history that make us blush, and the impotence of the Church in our own time that makes us blanch.

Nonetheless, our task is not to purge the tares. That

is God's business. He allows both to grow together until the harvest, lest plowing out the tares destroy also the wheat. The judgment will come each day, and on our last day. The basis of that judgment will be whether we have allowed the conviction of the saviorhood of Christ to become the experience of His Lordship in every facet of our lives.

But Jesus' parable offers hope. Because the wheat and the tares are allowed to coexist until harvest, we have time to determine whether we are wheat or tares. We know that tares can be transformed by God's grace into wheat before the harvest. The Lord leaves us with a question only we can decide. Am I a stalk of wheat or a tare? To seriously ask the question of ourselves and to answer it with unreserved commitment to Him is a sure sign that we are part of the wheat that is ready for harvest.

Kingdom Thinking

1. Reflect on the impact the Church has in today's society. Is any of it negative, placing stumbling blocks before unbelievers?

2. What are some positive actions you have seen believers take that have resulted in stumbling blocks to faith being removed before unbelievers?

3. In what way was Jesus said to be a stumbling block (see Rom. 9:30-33)?

Related Readings

Matthew 11:1-6 Romans 2:22-24 Colossians 4:3-6

Prayer to the King

I confess, dear Lord, that I need Your strength and wisdom and guidance every day in every way. Protect me from the pride that supposes I can be self-sufficient, and from the vanity that refuses to admit needs, not only in order for me to walk more closely with You, but also so I will not become a stumbling block to others. In Jesus' name, Amen.

52

Might in Miniature

SCRIPTURE READING:

The kingdom of heaven is like a mustard seed, which a man took and sowed in his field; and this is smaller than all other seeds; but when it is full grown, it is larger than the garden plants, and becomes a tree.

MATTHEW 13:31,32

Some time ago, I went into a sporting goods store. They had a special sale on survival kits for the wilderness camper. I looked through the supplies provided to stay alive when lost or out of touch with civilization. One booklet was particularly interesting to me. It was entitled, *Before You Give Up!* It contained ten things to do to survive.

Ever feel so lost or out of touch with God that you feel like giving up? Life has a way of tempting us to despair, to give up on people, relationships, projects, hopes and dreams; sometimes on ourselves. The parable of the mustard seed is a hope-filled survival kit. Jesus' answer to the temptation to give up is to depend on Him to survive.

Some of Jesus' disciples were tempted to give up. Was following the Master worth it? Would it make any difference? Could this carpenter from Nazareth pull it off? Was He truly the Messiah? Why was it taking so long to establish His kingdom? Could He really affect the powerful political structure of Rome or the ecclesiastical authority of Jerusalem?

We can empathize. Evil seems so virulent. Change takes so much patience. Progress is difficult and slow. Impatience breeds discouragement and self-incrimination. It's then that we say, "If I only had more faith! Things would be different if I had enough faith to face life's excruciatingly slow process. My faith just isn't big enough!" As if everything depended on the size of our faith, we spiral subjectively into misguided musings about our own adequacy. The bad mood that results drains our energy and spreads to the people around us like a contagious disease.

Jesus' answer to His disciples and to us is piercing and penetrating. His antidote for impatience rooted in our own impotence is this homely parable filled with holy truth and hope. "Before you give up," Jesus says, "consider the mustard seed."

The mustard seed plant was an herb often found in gardens in Palestine. One particular kind grew rapidly from a minute seed so small the naked eye could barely see it. Yet, it grew rapidly into a bush, then into a shrub the size of a tree. The result was a strong-branched growth in which birds could not only perch, but also build nests.

The Lord Himself is the "certain man," the sower of the mustard seed. The seed is His gift of faith in us. When that seed grows in us, we can be planted in the world as examples of what the power of God can do to heal discouragement. When we ourselves are tempted to become discouraged, we need to remember that it's not the size of our faith but the immensity of God's power that makes the difference.

Jesus' own life and ministry exemplified the meaning of the parable. God planted a seed in Bethlehem. He grew in wisdom and stature. Then He came forth proclaiming the kingdom of God. His message of love set people free. The Cross and the Resurrection followed. Pentecost and the birth of the Church unleashed His power. Incredible growth! The mustard tree of a universal movement stands as a powerful witness to the power of the original seed. A small beginning; a triumphant conclusion still to come. Surely the Early Church found great hope in the parable as it faced insurmountable odds with a faith that had removed mountains.

When Jesus told this parable, He wanted His disciples to dare to believe that what was happening before their eyes was the beginning of the transformation of the world. God was working out His purposes, and He could accomplish the same miracle of growth in them.

Christ lifts our inverted attention off our own insufficient faith to the immensity of God's resources for growth and change. All we are to do is receive the seed through the Holy Spirit and leave the results to God.

Put into focus the people, problems and responsibilities that cause you discouragement. The issue is not the size of your faith anymore than the light switch is electricity. Our only task is to flip the switch!

Kingdom Thinking

1. Reflect on the time you first came to a saving knowledge of Christ. Without boasting, but by way of encouragement, think of some specific areas in which you have grown spiritually since then.

2. Do particular instances or kinds of problems tempt you to become discouraged?

3. Name some specific disciplines, steps or exercises that can allow the power of God to loom larger in our minds and experience than our limited ideas of what can happen.

Related Readings

Matthew 14:22-31 1 Corinthians 10:13
Revelation 2:8-11

Prayer to the King

When we dwell on our own resources, O Lord, our faith wavers. But when we focus on Your power and love, we know You can cause our faith to move mountains. Save us from weak faith, as You save us from our sins. We pray in the name of Him in whom we believe, Amen.

53

Birds in the Bush

SCRIPTURE READING:

The kingdom of heaven is like a mustard seed, which...becomes a tree, so that the birds of the air come and nest in its branches.

MATTHEW 13:31,32

I had a difficult time going to sleep in the hotel room on a trip to the east coast. My body was on California time. After I had prayed my prayers and read for hours, sleep still eluded me. Finally I turned on the television set. Between the scenes of an old western movie, a 30-second spot appeared on the screen. It caught my attention. In bold letters was the message, "Before you give up, call 866-3242."

I wasn't about to give up anything except getting

some rest, but my interest was piqued. I dialed the number and found that it was a Christian crisis-intervention ministry. The woman's voice on the other end of the line spoke before I identified myself. "Before you give up, try Jesus! Can I be of any help?" I thanked her and told her that I was a Californian whose only problem was sleeplessness. She laughed, and we had a good conversation about her ministry to people who are about ready to give up.

As we noted in the previous chapter, that's what the parable of the mustard seed is about, too. Some of Jesus' disciples were about ready to give up, but we, too, have our own discouragements. Some people are ready to give up on their marriage after years of trying. Others are tempted to give up hope for a friend or loved one. Still others are discouraged because they feel that regardless of what they do to try to change things, nothing works.

The promise of this parable is not just that God is more powerful than our inadequacy, and can cause a tiny bit of faith to grow large; it is also that it can grow large enough to cause us to be communicators of hope to people around us who are ready to give up. The mustard seed grew into a tree large enough to attract birds who needed a place to rest. When we are mustard trees, we are able to remind others of the difference the Lord, and hope, can make in their lives.

I once preached at the Church of the Lepers in

Taipei, Taiwan. The work among these rejected people was begun by a great lady named Lillian Dixon. It is called the Mustard Seed Ministry. A tiny seed of trust has unleashed the infinite power of God. Lillian believed that God had called her to begin the work. She trusted Him completely. Money began coming in from all over the world and the work expanded. Now, the results tower like a great mustard tree. At times, Lillian had often been tempted to give up. But the Lord wanted to amaze the world with how many birds He could perch in her tree! When I saw the healed bodies and transformed personalities that have resulted, I myself was given new courage and hope.

Paul was very conscious that the numbers of people he was able to encourage in Christ was the result of the way the Lord had worked in his life. His faith had grown into a towering tree, compared to that first faltering confession on the Damascus road. In turn, he could encourage the Philippians: "For I am confident of this very thing, that He who began a good work in you will perfect it until the day of Christ Jesus" (Phil. 1:6). Paul could remind the Ephesians that although they had once been estranged from God, "You are no longer strangers and aliens, but you are fellow citizens with the saints, and are of God's household, having been built upon the foundation of the apostles and prophets, Christ Jesus Himself being the corner stone, in whom the whole building, being fitted together is growing into a holy temple in the Lord" (Eph. 2:19-21).

God is on the move in us. He wants to make us His miracle for the world to see what He can do. And He's not finished; He's barely begun. When we reflect on what God has done with the mustard seed of our first trusting response to the gospel, we can yield our troublesome affairs to Him. He is growing a mustard tree large enough to bless others. Be sure of that!

We are not expected to be perfect. We are expected to be contagious infusers of viable hope. There are discouraged people everywhere in our lives; they desperately need a mustard tree to perch on. That's the final twist of the parable. Once God grows a mustard tree out of our seed of faith, the worried birds will flock there to receive what we have discovered.

Kingdom Thinking

1. Has there ever been a time in your life when someone served as a "mustard tree," encouraging you and providing a "branch" on which you could rest?

2. Are you experiencing any discouragement now that you could share with others, allowing them to become a "mustard tree" for you?

3. How can the Church become more effective in providing a means of discovering needs, and serving as an encouraging, empowering fellowship?

Related Readings

Isaiah 40:28-31 2 Corinthians 1:3-7 Hebrews 12:12,13

Prayer to the King

Dear Lord, help us not only to be concerned about our own faith, but also to be ready to encourage faith in others. Help us to remember that, like love, our own faith grows by being given away. Above all, help us to trust in You above the quality of our own faith or performance. Through Christ our Lord, Amen.

54

Changing from the Inside Out

SCRIPTURE READING:

He spoke another parable to them, "The kingdom of heaven is like leaven, which a woman took, and hid in three pecks of meal, until it was all leavened."

MATTHEW 13:33

"It's changed my personality!" This was the confident claim of a middle-aged entertainer who had just had a face-lift. She had gone to a world-renowned cosmetic surgeon. His artistry removed the lines that age and difficulties had plowed deeply into her cheeks. The bags under her eyes were gone; the furrows in her brow had been stretched smooth.

"You look like a new woman!" I said, in affirmation of the pain and expense she had endured.

"I only hope I can stay that way!" she responded, in a concerned voice that contradicted her now smooth, china-doll face. Then she explained that the surgeon had told her that the face is an expression of the psyche, and that her face-lift would last only if there were a change in her inner patterns of thought and emotions—in her personality.

Personality change is not easy. Most authorities say that once a person's personality is set by early training, example and molding, it cannot be changed. Jesus shows us otherwise. He can transform our personalities! He never used the word. And yet, everything He said, did and does, radically alters and reshapes personality. He has called us to be His people in order to remold us in His own image, and then send us into life as liberated personalities. The parable of the leaven is the parable of the transformation of personality and, subsequently, the transforming power of a Christ-centered personality.

Leaven was a little piece of dough kept over from a previous baking. (Bread makers today call it "starter.") While it was stored, it fermented. After a time, it was ready to be kneaded into a new batch of dough. It pervaded the entire dough with its transforming influence. The dough would change its nature and size through the silent, rising impact of the leaven.

The leaven of Christ enters our lives when we accept the love and forgiveness He offers us. We know that we are accepted just as we are, but He will not leave us there. Once the leaven of His presence enters our lives, it begins to reorganize the total dough of the person we are—from the inside out. Everything is touched by the insistent infusion. Christ's persistent love pervades and penetrates our total person. *That* he has taken charge of us is comforting; *how* He transforms us is often very uncomfortable.

First, He enables us to enjoy the strengths of our personalities. Then He penetrates into the attitudes, experiences and habit patterns that cripple our growth and debilitate our relationships with others. All of the eccentric traits that reveal we are off center, away from Him, are exposed one by one. The Potter of personality reveals how we would look, sound and act if those traits were surrendered to Him.

The leaven works inadvertently. The more we focus our total attention on the leavening Lord Himself, the more we become like Him. That's the exciting adventure of Christian growth. The indwelling Lord is up to nothing less than making us like Himself! Our task is not to try to develop Christian virtues, but to yield ourselves to Christ. The virtues of Christlikeness will then grow naturally.

Frequently I hear people say, "If I could get out of the way, if I could only get rid of self, I would be more of the Christian I was meant to be." That's absurd! It's like the dough refusing to be dough. Just as every particle of the dough is transformed by the leaven, so our lives are transformed by the indwelling Lord. He is in us and we in Him. No one would dissect rising dough to discern what is the dough and what is the leaven. The two are so inseparably intermingled that the union is imperceptible. The issue is the ever-expanding scope of Christ's penetration in our personality.

The process is facilitated by taking a personal inventory of our personalities, and asking what aspects need changing. Then we engage in creatively introspective prayer. We ask the Lord to give us a picture of what His leavening wants to liberate us to be. It's helpful to keep a logbook with your Bible and to make a list of areas of your personality where the leaven needs to work. Record daily what you experience of the Lord's changes in your personality. You will be amazed; the people around you will be delighted—and thankful!

Kingdom Thinking

1. How would you describe your personality? (Outgoing or introspective, intense or "laid back," thoughtful or activist, etc.)

2. How would the people closest to you describe your personality? (Note any differences between 1 and

2—your own perception, and that of others. What makes the discrepancy?)

3. List five assets of your personality.

4. If you could change any aspect of your personality, what would it be? (What aspects are liabilities?) If Christ were to write a critique of your personality, what would He write?

Related Readings

Romans 12:1-3 2 Corinthians 3:12-18
2 Corinthians 5:14-17

Prayer to the King

Dear Lord, I long to be reshaped into the same image of Your Son. Yet, because You have already had a hand in shaping who I am, help me not to be so dissatisfied with myself that I am insecure or artificial. Just grant me an openness to the working of Your leaven in my life. Through Jesus Christ our Lord, Amen.

55

Leavening the Lump

SCRIPTURE READING:

He spoke another parable to them, "The kingdom of heaven is like leaven, which a woman took, and hid in three pecks of meal, until it was all leavened."

MATTHEW 13:33

The parable of the leaven is both about the power of God in transforming us personally and, subsequently, about the transforming power of a Christ-centered personality. As He leavens our personalities, He also sends us into life as a leavening influence. What He does for us personally is in preparation for what He wants to do through us in the world.

Even the Master's own incarnation was an example of the leavening power of God being kneaded into the dough of humanity. His life would alter the shape of history. Imperceptibly at first, then undeniably. Jesus was the fullness of God, infusing new life and beginning a new creation. He brought an entirely new element into life: the gospel of the kingdom of God, the reign and rule of God in all of life. Christ's life and message was the insertion of the leaven; His death infused its power; His resurrection released its pervading dynamic; His presence in the Holy Spirit is now permeating the whole of life. The bread is rising!

Kingdom people are the leaven of the kingdom of God in society. The individual is always the key. The whole dough of humanity is made up of its separate parts. The leaven transforms every particle of the dough. That means you and me! The Lord then uses us to leaven society.

The adventure of working with people is maximized for me because I can share the pilgrimage of personality transformation with them. The most exciting times in my life are when I can be part of the Lord's implantation of the leaven in people. It's a delight to watch people change and grow after they have entered the Kingdom and allowed the reign and rule of Christ to be the leaven in their personalities.

What Christ has been in us as the leaven, we are to be in the world. Our influence in the lives of others is like Christ's influence in us: pervasive, penetrating and permeating. As His leaven pervades each aspect of our inner person or personality, the result should be manifest for others to see. We should be the source of repeated questions: How did you get the way you are? How can I find what you have found?

This makes our evaluation of the extent Christ is evident in our personalities a crucial issue. A negative, cold, unloving personality is a contradiction of terms. Not everyone is endowed with physical attractiveness. But each of us is capable of becoming an attractive personality. Christ's love and warmth can do that for all of us.

Our personality is our window to the world. People will be able to see what can happen to them by observing what is happening to us. Leaven is observable only as it is working, not after the bread is baked. Our task is not to become "perfect," but to expose the leaven as it is working in us. As we share what the Lord is doing as well as what He has done, we will make contact with other struggling persons. Vulnerability and openness create contagious communication about the adventure of the Spirit's transforming work.

No more vivid and dramatic illustration of this process exists than Saul of Tarsus, who became the apostle Paul. He refers to the transforming power of God in his own life in almost all of his epistles to the Early Church. Then, wherever he went, the apostle introduced others to the Savior, and encouraged them to be open to the same leavening Lord he had experienced. To the Colossians, he wrote that when the Word of Christ dwelt in them richly, it would impact others: they would have an outer personality of compassion, kindness, humility, gentleness, forbearance, forgiveness and encouragement (see Col. 3:12-17).

The parable of the leaven is both confrontation and cheer. It confronts us with what Christ wants to do in our lives, and cheers us with the good news that no one of us needs to remain as he is! Where is the leaven at work in you right now? For whom have you been called to be the agent of leavening? Christ will not be finished until He has transformed every part of us, every person around us and all of society.

Has anyone asked you lately how you came to be the way you are?

Kingdom Thinking

1. How do "vulnerability and openness" relate to our being able to be a leavening influence in the lives of others?

2. Can you identify someone who has been a "leavening" influence in your life?

3. Assessing your own gifts, in what ways do you think you might best spread the Lord's leavening to others?

4. What factors among the Christian Church at large do you think may inhibit its being a more forceful leavening influence in the world?

Related Readings

Acts 9:17-22 Colossians 3:12-17 2 Peter 2:9-12

Prayer to the King

We praise You, dear Lord, for changing our hearts and leavening our lives with Your love and grace. Help us in turn to be gracious people, living testimony to Your power to work wonders in the human heart, winsome witnesses of Your rule and reign. In the name of Jesus we pray, Amen.

56

The God of Experience and the Experience of God

SCRIPTURE READING:

And they said to Him, "The disciples of John often fast and offer prayers; the disciples of the Pharisees also do the same; but Yours eat and drink." And Jesus said to them, "You cannot make the attendants of the bridegroom fast while the bridegroom is with them, can you? But the days will come; and when the bridegroom is taken away from them, then they will fast in those days."

LUKE 5:33-35

There's a great difference between the God of our experience and our experience of God. The opponents of Jesus had a God of history. He had revealed His nature in crucial events and pronouncements, and the scribes and Pharisees had added their own customs that had become the basis of the Hebrew religion. The tragedy is that they were locked in on the firm belief that the God who had spoken in the past was not speaking in their own age.

The battle lines had been drawn in Luke 5:17, when they came to investigate Jesus' ministry and discovered that He had the audacity to forgive the sins of a paralyzed man. "Who can forgive sins, but God alone?" (v. 21) they asked. The tension increased when Jesus called a member of an abhorred trade, a tax collector named Levi, to follow Him (see v. 27). "Why do you eat and drink with the tax-gatherers and sinners?" (v. 30) they asked. And now they are offended because Jesus' disciples did not fast, as they expected. He responds with a little-known parabolic saying about fasting, all three incidents leading up to the better-known sayings about garments and wineksins in verses 36-39.

In Jesus' day, a full week of celebration occurred following a wedding. Everyone who attended was relieved of all religious observances that would lessen the delightful merriment. The messianic age would be like that. Jesus the Bridegroom had ushered in a time of unprecedented blessing from God. It was no time for the solemn ritual of fasting! There would be plenty of time for that after He was taken away.

In these incidents, the Lord contradicted the leaders' experience of God in three drastic ways. First, He affirmed the contemporary presence of the authority to forgive sins, vested in Himself as the Son of man. Then, He asserted the inclusiveness of God's love by calling a tax gatherer to the table with Him. And, finally, He identified Himself as the Bridegroom at the Messianic feast, the One whose disciples could hardly be expected to fast.

Jesus showed in all these ways that God was doing a new thing in Him as the Messiah. He was more concerned about the needs of people than about the ancient rules and regulations. But the presuppositions of His opponents—their preoccupation with what God had done in the past—prevented them from experiencing what He was doing in the present. They did not expect new acts of intervention from the Almighty. The Law and all the annotated rules that applied the commandments to life were all they needed. Customs such as fasting had become an obsession, and the fastidious practice of their rituals had become a replacement for intimate, present communion with God Himself.

But don't we often have a similar problem? Many Christians can recount with elaborate detail how they first discovered God's grace in some experience of need or challenge. Often, the treasured memory of the past becomes more important than what God wants to do in the present. But faith is dynamic, not static. God wants us to be open and receptive to new truths about Him and fresh encounters with Him in our daily lives. Whatever has happened to us is only a prelude to what He is about to do. There's never a time when we can rest on our past experience of Him, never an excuse for complacency. The Lord is always on the move.

Yet, something in all of us longs for the tragic tranquility of memories rather than forward movement. We resist the penetration of the Spirit of God into untouched areas of our personalities and habits. We want to say, "Lord, I've learned enough for a while. I know who You are and what You have done. Just allow me to enjoy life as it is, without any new crises or difficulties that force me to change and grow!"

Many of us have built a whole theology on our personal experiences of God. But our experiences can come to build us. We must realize that God's question to us is not whether He has been important to us in the past. His question is, "What have you allowed me to teach you and give you and do for you lately?"

Kingdom Thinking

1. What new discovery, experience or growth has taken place in your faith in the past month?
2. How has your fresh experience of God changed

your relationship with Him? From your own experience, what's the difference between the God of your past experience and the experience of God?

3. What kinds of hindrances can arise that may cause us to be unable to accept new things God wants to do in our lives? What can we do about them?

Related Readings

Isaiah 43:18-21 Acts 2:14-21 Philippians 3:7-14

Prayer to the King

O God, our help in ages past, help us to be open also to Your continuing works in days to come. Grant that we may not allow our experience of You in the past to make us think You are predictable or limited in what You can do today. Help us not to become so comfortable with the familiar that we miss Your continuing work in the world, and in our lives, today. In Christ's name we pray, Amen.

57

The Adventure of Faith

SCRIPTURE READING:

No one tears a piece from a new garment and puts it on an old garment; otherwise he will both tear the new, and the piece from the new will not match the old.

LUKE 5:36

Fellowship with God is an adventure that is never completed. He is never finished with us; therefore, we are never finished growing. He is engaged in a momentous transformation in each of us. We have hardly begun to become the person He is ready and able to liberate us to be.

The parable of the new patch on an old garment

exposes the inadequacy of not being open to this God who is on the move in our lives. Jesus was telling His opponents that their experience of God was like an old garment. It could not bear the strain of the new revelation God was giving them through His Son. The new cloth simply did not match the old. They needed a new garment, not a patched old one.

We cannot patch up our old self with a fragment of the gospel. The imagery of clothes and clothing in the Scriptures makes the idea all the more impelling. The Lord came, lived and died to clothe us with the righteousness of God. Paul reflected on what our response should be: "Put on the new self, which in the likeness of God has been created in righteousness and holiness of the truth" (Eph. 4:24). "Put on a heart of compassion, kindness, humility, gentleness and patience" (Col. 3:12). The wardrobe of a new person in Christ is not tattered, patched and restyled. It is new—made of the character of Christ Himself.

God is the original innovator. The verb form of *kainos*, the Greek word for "new" in this parable, means to make new or to make afresh, as if new. Each new day of life brings opportunities to feel the freshness of His love. He can take our most ordinary situations and make them into occasions for the innovative things He wants to do in us. Our God has all power, resources and people at His disposal to break through our defenses with possibilities we never dreamed possible. All He needs from us is an openness expressed by spreading all of our problems, relationships and responsibilities before Him. At this very moment, He is preparing the innovation that will bring a solution or answer that no amount of cleverness or planning on our part could have devised. And this dynamic nowness of God demands newness from His people. A patch on an old garment will not do.

Life is filled with predictably unpredictable events. We can never freeze-frame God and be sure that He has nothing new to teach us about Himself or about us. The moment we think we have captured all the "unsearchable riches" of His nature, He breaks out of our carefully fashioned old garment. True, He is "the same yesterday, today, and tomorrow," but all that He is takes eternity to realize. A special joy is given to "What's next, Lord?" teachable saints. The unfolding drama of life is for the unveiling of aspects of His nature that we will never learn if we become comfortably settled on dead center.

I know this to be true in my own life. When I am finished with my careful categories of how God deals with me and am sure that the best He has to give has been given, He forces me to face my spiritual immaturity by giving me an opportunity or problem that is so far beyond my strength that I am amazed I could ever have been satisfied with my previous relationship with Him.

The God of my previous experience is constantly in

competition with my fresh experiences of Him. But He will not allow me to break the first commandment and have other gods before Him—not even the idol of my dependence on the old garments of the past. I have discovered that my tenacious hold on reflections of great experiences of the past is really fear of the future. The false security of the familiar must constantly be replaced with the new garments of trusting God with the complexities and uncertainties staring me in the face today.

Once the Lord takes up residence in us, a dynamic process begins by which everything is made new. He reorders the tissues of our brains so we can think His thoughts. Memories are healed and liberated. Values and purposes are reoriented. Our image of ourselves is transformed. He is satisfied with nothing less than molding us into His own image. The miracle of the new creation never stops. The old person in us is made a new person. Can we be satisfied with anything less than a new garment?

Kingdom Thinking

1. In your experience in the Church, what "old garments" have become strait jackets that hinder flexibility?

2. Can you cite any breakthroughs when you have been released from old habits or ways of thinking, or

when new ideas have liberated you from previous bondage and set you on the road to fresh, new growth in Christ?

3. What are some ways we can keep our faith flexible and our attitudes open for the innovative?

Related Readings

Ephesians 6:10-17 Colossians 3:9-14
Revelation 7:9-14

Prayer to the King

We praise You, God of the old and the new, for having made us priests and kings in Your kingdom, and clothing us in the new and unsoiled garments given us by Your Son. Help us never to rest complacently on the experiences of our yesterdays, but to be open to the freshness of Your tomorrows. Through Christ we pray, Amen.

58

The Taste of New Wine

SCRIPTURE READING:

And no one puts new wine into old wineskins; otherwise the new wine will burst the skins, and it will be spilled out, and the skins will be ruined. But new wine must be put into fresh wineskins.

LUKE 5:37,38

The opponents of Jesus should have been prepared for something as drastically different as the works of Jesus. Long ago, God had predicted through the prophet Isaiah,

> Behold, I will do something new,
> Now it will spring forth;

> Will you not be aware of it?
> I will even make a roadway in the
> wilderness,
> Rivers in the desert (Isa. 43:19).

Yet, the scribes and Pharisees resisted the new thing God was doing in Jesus. They were as rigid and inflexible as old wineskins.

In Jesus' day, wineskins were made by coating the skin of a goat with pitch and sealing it to make a bag. The neck was the opening; it was closed tightly after the new wine, freshly pressed from the grapes, was poured in. The fermentation process began. The new skin was soft and flexible, capable of taking the expanding, tumultuous fermentation process. It stretched as the wine fermented.

The reason an old bag could not contain the new wine was that it had already been stretched to capacity. It had become dry, cracked and inflexible. The fermentation process was sure to burst the skin, the bag would be destroyed and the wine lost.

Jesus tells His opponents that His incarnation as the Messiah is the new wine, while they are the old wineskins. He had new ways—indeed, a new covenant—that they could not contain unless they were willing to be transformed into wineskins as new as the Lord's new wine.

We wonder if Jesus had the words of Job on His

mind. "Behold my belly [heart] is like unvented wine, like new wineskins it is about to burst" (Job 32:19). Or was He thinking of the time when the representatives of Gibeon came to Joshua and pretended their depravity by their broken wineskins: "And these wineskins which we filled were new, and behold, they are torn; and these our clothes and our sandals are worn out because of the very long journey" (Josh. 9:13). We cannot be sure.

But what is certain is that the leaders of Israel were the wineskins Jesus had in mind. And us! Who can escape the incisive implication? Not I.

The Lordship of Jesus Christ cannot be poured into the old skin of our settled personality structure, presuppositions about life, prejudices about people, plans for the future and predetermined ideas of what He will do or how we will respond. The dry, cracked bags of the past will burst; we will lose our cherished religion and Him as well.

Make no mistake: Jesus Himself is the new wine. We could ask for no better gift than the gift of Himself. More than answers to our problems, we need the power of His presence. Our minds and hearts have been made for Him; we must keep them elastic enough to allow for the new things He does every day of our lives. This is the secret meaning of the parable of the new wineskins. We are to present to the Lord a fresh wineskin of viability each day and in each new situation. If we depend on previous experience alone, we will be like old wineskins that burst.

The parable of the wineskins is desperately needed in the Church today. Some of us have never experienced the taste of the new wine of the indwelling Christ. Our bags are empty. But many of us are about to burst because we have offered Christ a dry, cracked, used wineskin. We are disturbed by the demands of following Him in our inner hearts. We are offended at the people He invites to dine with Him, and the way He impels us into the problems of society.

All this leads me to a personal decision I hope you will share. I have learned a great deal through the study of Scripture and years of fellowship with the Lord. But I suspect that my most exciting years are ahead. How about you? If so, I want to surrender any false pride or dependence on the past and make a fresh beginning. My past experience of God can never substitute for the experience of God today.

Will you say with me, "Lord, here is a fresh wineskin; fill me"?

Kingdom Thinking

1. What factors make people resistant to change?

2. Describe from your own experience and observation of others what it's like to be an "old wineskin" and a "new wineskin."

3. What attitudes are required to present to the Lord a new wineskin each day?

4. How does the parable of the wineskins relate to the Church? to its leaders and members? its customs and forms of worship? What kinds of changes would be creative, and what kinds and methods of change would be destructive? What are our standards for dynamic renewal?

Related Readings

Acts 2:8-13 1 Corinthians 5:7,8 Revelation 21:1-5

Prayer to the King

Dear Father, we have felt the urge of the Pharisees to cling to old ways. Yet we also know the inadequacy of trying to house Your Spirit in rigid hearts and closed minds. Grant that we may be pliable without being weak, open without being gullible. Thank You for filling us with the wine of Your daily presence. Through Christ the living Lord, Amen.

59

All Leaf and No Fruit

SCRIPTURE READING:

And He began telling this parable: "A certain man had a fig tree which had been planted in his vineyard; and he came looking for fruit on it, and did not find any. And he said to the vineyard-keeper, 'Behold, for three years I have come looking for fruit on this fig tree without finding any. Cut it down! Why does it even use up the ground?'"

LUKE 13:6,7

What measurements would you use to evaluate the effectiveness of a church? What would you say distinguishes a great congregation? Many people would think of the size of the membership, the quality of the preaching, the vitality of the educational program or the building program, or the warmth of the fellowship.

The parable of the fig tree teaches us that the one test of a great church—or an effective life—is fruitfulness. This is one of Jesus' more difficult parables, not because it is obscure, but because it is so incisively direct. The fig tree represents Israel, who thought of herself both as a vineyard and as a planting. Both symbols are mingled in the parable of the fig tree. The owner of the vineyard is God, and the vineyard keeper is Jesus. We are permitted to overhear the divine dialogue as the keeper implores the expectant owner to give the tree more time to bear fruit.

In Mark's account, the parable is set and dramatized in Jesus' final days in Jerusalem. Jesus noticed a fig tree with leaves—but only leaves. That's more than a horticultural observation. Leaves on a fig tree never precede the fruit. They sometimes accompany, but usually follow, the fruit. Seeing the leaves, Jesus would expect to find figs. In this case, however, all the life of the tree had run to the leaf, and in a focused moment of divine impatience Jesus cursed it (see Mark 11:12-14). When He and His disciples passed by the next morning, it was withered to the roots. Jesus offers an admonition more than an explanation: "Have faith in God" (v. 22).

At first we wonder what this has to do with a barren and withered fig tree. Then it dawns on us: after all of God's patient tending, Israel was lacking in faith.

The outward forms of her religion signified the historic knowledge and experience of God, but Jesus found only the leaves of pretension. Rites, rules, regulations and restrictions had become more important than the fruit of personal faith. Jesus was concerned about the "weightier matters of the law, justice and mercy and faith" (Matt. 23:23, *RSV*). What Jesus looked for could not be accomplished without a dependent trust in God.

Jesus talked a lot about fruitfulness throughout His ministry. False prophets can be identified by their fruits; grapes are not gathered from thorn bushes, nor figs from thistles; every good tree bears good fruit, but the rotten tree bears bad fruit. Every tree that does not bear good fruit is cut down and destroyed (see Matt. 7:15-21). Jesus' judgment on Israel was that although they were the tree of God, they had produced only the leaves of religion—the external appearances—but not the fruit of righteousness in individuals and the nation as a whole.

That last week in Jerusalem precipitated a direct confrontation with the Jewish officialdom. When Jesus raised Lazarus from the dead, rode triumphantly into Jerusalem and cleansed the Temple, the battle lines were drawn. The fig tree focused the issue for Jesus. His response to the fruitless, unproductive tree enacted the divine indignation and impatience with irrelevant, entrenched religion. The outward forms of religion were not bad in themselves, but they were to be a result of faith, not a replacement of it. The leaves had become more important than the fruit.

It would be fine if we could end our exposition with historical reflection about Israel. But the message is timeless. It speaks to the Church in every age. The danger of leaves without fruit is ever present. Today, our buildings, mass choirs, magnificent educational programs and religious organizations mean little if no real fruit results.

But the parable is also personal, as it raises a question about each of us. Unless our prayers, churchmanship and activity produce fruit, we are in danger of being cut off. The intercession of the vineyard keeper gives both comfort and urgency. "Give the tree one more year!" We have another chance.

Kingdom Thinking

1. What is the church where you fellowship best known for? its building? its youth program? its preaching? Do you think its *fruitfulness* matches its reputation? How can any gaps be closed?

2. Ask similar questions of your own life as a Christian. What image do you think others have of you (what "leaves" do they see)? In what ways do you think you could be a more consistent fruit bearer?

Related Readings

Psalm 80:8-11,14-16 Isaiah 5:1-7 Matthew 23:23-26

Prayer to the King

We know the value of the visible, O Father, and we are encouraged by public demonstrations of the faith. But help us also to perceive the vanity of externals alone. Grant that we may both attract others by being Your flourishing tree, and provide those who are attracted with substance and nourishment and godly fruit. In Jesus' name, Amen.

60

Abiding Fruitfulness

SCRIPTURE READING:

And he said to the vineyard-keeper,... "Why does it [this tree] even use up the ground?" And he answered and said to him, "Let it alone, sir, for this year too, until I dig around it and put in fertilizer; and if it bears fruit next year, fine; but if not, cut it down."

LUKE 13:7-9

We have seen the folly of a church or an individual Christian being all leaf and no fruit. But what do we mean by bearing fruit? What is true fruitfulness for us today? And what is the source of nourishment that produces the fruit we are to bear?

The answer lies in what Christ wants us to do with our gifts, and what He wants to do through us as our source of nourishment. Fruitfulness is never one without the other. The fruit we bear is our responsibility toward others, but that can be done only as we experience His life force coursing through our corporate and individual lives.

Both aspects are captured in Jesus' message on fruitfulness in John 15. It was the night before Jesus was crucified. What He said to them is our guide to a fruitful life. The motive and method of fruitfulness are expressed in a powerful little word: *abide*. We are to abide in Christ, and to invite Him to abide in us:

> Abide in Me, and I in you. As the branch cannot bear fruit of itself, unless it abides in the vine, so neither can you, unless you abide in Me. I am the vine, you are the branches; he who abides in Me, and I in him, he bears much fruit; for apart from Me you can do nothing (John 15:4,5).

The Greek word for abide is *meno*. Its rich meanings include to dwell, remain and rest. It also implies continuing in a relationship, faithful and unchanging. It means to sojourn, tarry and to wait. Most of all, it means to remain *continuously*. When we abide in Christ, we appropriate all He has done for us. That means unreserved acceptance of His death for our sins and His resurrection for the defeat of all the enemies of the abundant life. We abide in Christ when we accept His love as our assurance, His forgiveness as our freedom and His presence as our power. Fruitfulness has no beginning if it does not begin by abiding—trusting completely in Christ for our salvation and our eternal life.

But this is only the beginning. We were created for Christ to abide in us. He is the indwelling Lord in the contemporary power of the Holy Spirit. When we commit our lives to Him, we become the post-Pentecost abiding, dwelling place of the Lord. This is the secret of fruitfulness. From within, He begins His transforming work.

The apostle John clarifies this in his first epistle to the churches. He writes to assure Christians that they have been born of God because His seed abides in them (see 1 John 3:9). Through the seed of Christ in us, God's nature, revealed in Jesus, is reproduced in us. This means that our thoughts, temperament and disposition are being remolded in Christlikeness. The progression is exciting: we are born of God, chosen and called. We abide in His love for us in Christ, and He abides in us for the transformation of our character. The fruit of Christ indwelling is the new you, recreated as a new creature in Christ.

This is what Paul meant when he talked about the fruits of the Spirit. Christ's Spirit, abiding in us, manifests the character of Christ through us. Here, then, is personal fruitfulness as the result of Christ making us like Himself: love, joy, peace, patience, kindness, goodness, faithfulness, gentleness and self-control (see Gal. 5:22). These are the "figs" the Lord wants to grow on the tree of our lives. None is available apart from Him. We can inventory our fruitfulness by evaluating the evidence of the fruits of His Spirit.

This presses us on to the fruit He wants to produce through us in others. "This is My commandment, that you love one another, just as I have loved you" (John 15:12). How has He loved us? The next verse answers our question: "Greater love has no one than this, that one lay down his life for his friends." There it is! Fruitfulness is loving people as we have been loved—with giving, forgiving, sacrificial love. The test of fruitfulness is laying down our lives for others, and the reproduction of our faith in their faithful lives.

But catch the wonder of it all: The fruit our Lord demands, He graciously imputes as His gift!

Kingdom Thinking

1. Have you ever known anyone who seems to have all the right external signs or fruits of Christianity, but seems to be lacking in its true inner Spirit? What does Jesus call such people (see Matt. 23:23,24)?

2. What actions on God's part correspond to the

extra time and effort the vineyard keeper wanted to be expended on the barren tree (see Acts 3:24-26)?

3. In the church where you fellowship, is the emphasis on the minister or other professional staff bearing the primary responsibility for the church's bearing fruit, or on the need for the membership at large to reproduce the fruits of the Spirit in themselves and others? What can be done to heighten the latter emphasis?

4. The fruit of a Christian is introducing others to Christ. Why can so few church people identify others whom they have led to Him?

Related Readings

John 15:6-8 Galatians 5:22-26 2 Peter 1:5-8

Prayer to the King

Dear Lord, we want to be fruitful trees in Your garden, not barren. We confess that without Your Son indwelling our lives, we can do nothing. Help us to catch a vision of what fruit we can bear when we abide in Him, and He in us. Thank you for granting to us the capacity to bear the fruit You require! Through Jesus Christ our Lord, Amen.

Discussion Leader's Guide

This book is not only useful as a devotional guide, but also as a resource for a discussion and/or fellowship group. The following guidelines will help you organize and conduct a series of regular meetings for a variety of groups. If this book is used as the curriculum of a church-school class series, the following suggestions may be utilized for the discussion period following a teacher's presentation of the material.

It may be helpful to introduce a series of group sessions by reading the introduction to the book. Be sure class members understand the basic concept of the kingdom of God as the rule or reign of God "within you" (Luke 17:20,21, *NKJV*)—not just an event in the future. Explain also that these vignettes on living in the Kingdom are gleaned from the parables of Jesus.

How large should your group be? Ten to fifteen people make a good size for a discussion group. A smaller group may make continuity a problem when a few members are absent, while a larger group makes it difficult for everyone to participate. A large church-school class may be divided into smaller groups for discussion.

How often will you meet? Continuity is also a problem if the group meets less frequently than once a week. If you are leading a group that already meets regularly, such as a church-school class, decide how many weeks to spend on the series. Note that the sixty chapters of this book could provide more than a year's worth of once-a-week discussions. If this is too long to be realistic, a shorter period may be selected. For example, if you choose a twelve-week series, suggest that the members of the group read five chapters prior to each meeting and come prepared to discuss them. You may want to emphasize a group of particular chapters you have selected to be the focus of your discussion, but encourage people to read all five chapters for the meeting. Be sure to plan for any holidays that may come during the time you schedule the group's meetings.

You will also find a few questions for discussion at the end of each reading under the heading, "Kingdom Thinking." Of course, these are meant only to be suggestive. If you expect the group to last more than forty-five minutes to an hour, you will want to use more than one reading with its questions, or to supplement the suggested questions with more of your own. Don't overlook the way the class members' own questions can contribute to the relevance of the material to their own lives.

You, or someone you appoint, might act as group organizer, inviting others and perhaps calling class members to remind them of meeting dates, times and places.

Think about details such as whether refreshments will be served and whether child care should be arranged. In most cases, people will put more into the group—and get more out of it—if they are responsible for buying their own copy of the book and reading the entire book during the span of your series.

Most of the Scriptures referred to in the book are printed out, but it will still be helpful to ask group members to bring their own Bibles. It may also be useful to have a concordance in case someone brings up a related Scripture and the exact biblical reference is needed. A Bible dictionary can also be handy, although you will want to avoid transforming a series of devotional discussions into an impersonal study.

Be aware of basic principles of group dynamics, such as:

1. Arrange seating in a semicircle, the leader included instead of standing in front. This allows the setting to invite participation.
2. The following tips are helpful in guiding discussions:

    a. Accept statements from group members without judgmentalism, even if you disagree with them. If they are clearly unbiblical or unfair, you can ask questions or comment in a way that clarifies the issue; but outright rejection of people's thoughts is a good way to stifle open participation.

b. If a question or comment is off the subject, either suggest that it be dealt with at another time or ask the group members if they would prefer to pursue the new issue now.

c. If someone talks too much, direct a few questions specifically to someone else. Or, tactfully interrupt the person dominating the discussion by saying something like, "Excuse me, that's a good thought, and I wonder what some of the rest of us think about that." Sometimes you can talk with the person privately and enlist his or her help in drawing others into the discussion.

d. Make it easy and comfortable for everyone to share or ask questions, but don't force anyone to do so. Sometimes reluctant participants can warm to the idea of sharing by being asked to read a passage from the book. Sometimes it is helpful to divide the group into pairs or fours to discuss a particular question and report back to the group as a whole. Ask reluctant participants to write down a conclusion of the smaller group to be shared with the larger group.

e. If someone asks you a question and you don't know the answer, admit it and move on.

If the question calls for insight from personal experience, invite others to comment on it. If it requires special knowledge, offer to look for an answer in the library or from a counselor or pastor, and report later on your findings.

3. Unless the group leader is a therapist or other professional trained in counseling, guard against trying to do "group therapy." This doesn't mean that poignant moments won't come up or that difficult problems won't be raised, but the group is for sharing, not for in-depth counseling. The leader should be open and honest about wanting to grow with the group instead of coming across as someone who has all the answers.
4. Start and stop on time, according to the schedule agreed on before the series begins, for the benefit of people's own schedules.
5. Pray regularly for the sessions and the participants. God will honor your willingness to guide people toward a closer relationship with the King, and a more faithful walk under His rule.